WOMEN PLAYWRIGHTS
The Best Plays of 1997

Editor's Note

Women Playwrights: The Best Plays of 1997 is the sixth volume in the Best Plays by Women Playwrights series initiated by Smith and Kraus in 1992.

Each year we consider plays, written by American Women, that have premiered during that year's theatrical season. Submissions are made on a continuous basis by playwrights, agents, literary managers, and theatres.

Next year's book, *Women Playwrights: The Best Plays of 1998,* will include plays that premiered between September 1, 1997 and August 31, 1998.

—*Marisa Smith*

Marisa Smith has edited

Women Playwrights: The Best Plays of 1992
Women Playwrights: The Best Plays of 1993
Women Playwrights: The Best Plays of 1994
Women Playwrights: The Best Plays of 1995
Women Playwrights: The Best Plays of 1996

Act One Festival '95: The One-Act Plays
Act One Festival '95: The One-Act Plays

EST Marathon '94: The One-Act Plays
EST Marathon '95: The One-Act Plays
EST Marathon '96: The One-Act Plays
EST Marathon '97: The One-Act Plays

Humana Festival '93: The Complete Plays
Humana Festival '94: The Complete Plays
Humana Festival '95: The Complete Plays

WOMEN PLAYWRIGHTS

The Best Plays of 1997

CONTEMPORARY PLAYWRIGHTS
SERIES

SK
A Smith and Kraus Book

A Smith and Kraus Book
Published by Smith and Kraus, Inc.
PO Box 127, Lyme, NH 03768

First Edition: August 1998
10 9 8 7 6 5 4 3 2 1

The Library of Congress Cataloging-In-Publication Data
Women playwrights : the best plays of 1997 / edited by Marisa Smith
     p.   cm. — (Contemporary playwrights series)
     ISBN 1-57525-131-0
     1. American drama—women authors. 2. American drama—20th century. 3. Women—drama.
     I. Smith, Marisa. II. Series: Contemporary playwrights series.
     PS628.W6W668   1994
     812'.540809287—dc20
                   94-10071
                    CIP

CONTENTS

INTRODUCTION

It is time to stop asking if there is a feminine aesthetic. There are all kinds of aesthetics, and there always have been. Why shouldn't there be a feminine aesthetic? The question to ask is, *Will the feminine dramatic aesthetic survive?*

Plays written by women, like plays written by men, begin with a gender-derived set of assumptions about how the world works. This is not to say that all plays by women are alike, or that women only like or understand plays by women. This is simply to say that as women we are a culture, and when we start to write, we start at the same place. Perhaps one day, gender and other cultural differences will disappear, and the voice of a *white, woman* playwright will sound just like that of a *Haitian male* playwright and gender will no longer matter. But I doubt it.

For a long time I resisted this idea, as did many women who write for the theatre. Perhaps we feared that acknowledging the feminine aesthetic would isolate us, or cause us to seem less important than men playwrights. We resented the fact that nobody asked men playwrights if they had an aesthetic, and we grew tired of the question. But, in fact, the more plays I see by women, the clearer the feminine aesthetic becomes. And far from suggesting the sameness of men and women, women's plays point out the profound social, chemical, and biological differences between men and women.

For example, on the simplest possible level, men write plays about the search for home, while women write about the inevitable loss of it. Men write about loss, too, of course, but loss always seems to take men by surprise, whereas women know to expect it. In the masculine aesthetic, the loss is the event at the center of the play. For women, the event is how the loss is dealt with, how the mess is cleaned up, what is said and by whom, what is destroyed, what is born. In plays written by women, characters need more than anything else to figure out what the loss means.

Unfortunately, *Figuring out what something means* is not always recognized as an event, and wonderful plays by women are often rejected by producers because they don't seem to have the required event at the center of them. The remarkable plays in this volume have struggled to come to life in a marketplace that is still dominated by the masculine aesthetic. And they have succeeded. They are poetic and true.

These plays represent the feminine aesthetic at its highest. The main characters are not sitting around, hoping against hope, waiting for the happy ending. They are assessing their situation, identifying what they have lost, and securing what they have left. But it is not property or status women are concerned with losing. Almost always, loss, for women, is the loss of someone, a lover, a friend, a mother, a father, a child. To look at these plays, you might think that women had no concern whatsoever with things.

In the haunting work, *Defying Gravity*, by Jane Anderson, a young girl loses her mother in the explosion of the Challenger. Characters from far flung regions of time and place gather to stand with young Elizabeth as they count down the days to blastoff. Her mother says to her students, "People always believed that if you defied gravity, you were that much closer to God." But Elizabeth knows there is also a terrible price for defying gravity, because she and her mother have paid it. She is angry and she is alone. She doesn't ask for our sympathy. She warns us, though, that what is true for her will one day be true for us.

In *Tatjana in Color*, by Julia Jordan, a young girl is drawn to a diffident older artist, and is initiated by him into the world she will call her own, the world of color. Seeming at first glance a sexy coming of age play, *Tatjana* finally reveals itself to be a bold study in the steps between innocence and knowing, between waking and sleep.

Analiese, by Lynne Alvarez, is a dark and compelling folktale in which a young girl runs away, following her first love into the frozen north, only to find that, "this is no place to be free." Each person she meets she thinks will be her savior. But none of them are, of course. Love is not as simple as she thought it is: "too treacherous a journey for the fainthearted."

The House of Bernarda Alba, adapted by Emily Mann from a story by Federico Garcia Lorca, is a cautionary tale in which an imperial mother loses her youngest daughter in a vain attempt to control everything from the lives of her daughters to the passage of time. Everything around her has changed, and she has the opportunity to change too, now that her husband has died. But she doesn't. She won't. At the end of the play, she claims not to have lost, but she has.

My point about the feminine aesthetic is most clearly visible in this piece. As written by Garcia Lorca, the tale ends with the loss, with the discovery of the dead girl. Being a woman, I wanted more of this story. I wanted to know what happened the next day and the next. I wanted to know what the mother was going to make of this in a week or so, what the other daughters were going to do. As it is, the play is deep and rich, a carefully wrought tribute to a magnificent story. Small wonder I wasn't ready for it to end.

In Regina Taylor's *Escape from Paradise,* Jenine, a young writer recovering from a miscarriage, buys a ticket for Venice, hoping to leave everything behind. Over and over again in her life, the things she has chased after have become, by morning, "dead fireflies rolling around in the bottom of the jar." Jenine concludes, "It seems that it's not in the arrival—and holding onto; it's in the journey." This is the heart of the feminine dramatic aesthetic. Life flows through us and on. Any attempt to stop it, change it, or deny it is hopeless. Whatever joy is to be found must come from the hopelessness itself. Even so, there is considerable joy to be found.

I salute these five gifted writers and congratulate the publishers on the creation of this volume. It is the kind of offering that may actually assist in the survival of the feminine aesthetic. The survival of that aesthetic, and the women writers who express it, will insure that women's actual lives and their actual feelings about their lives, will make it into the permanent record of our time. We have been represented too long as we are perceived from the outside, not as we are known from within.

As the species needs both men and women in order to continue, so does the society, and the world of the arts that documents that society. These five women playwrights are to be treasured, supported, and produced. Do not read their work with a disinterested eye. Read these plays asking what you can do to help these writers remain in the forefront of the American theatre.

—Marsha Norman
Spring 1998

ANALIESE

Lynne Alvarez

To Craig, my dearest colleague.

THE AUTHOR

Lynne Alvarez arrived in New York in 1978 planning to be a hot shot poet. On a whim, she accompanied a friend to a gathering of Hispanic writers at the Puerto Rican Travelling Theatre. At thirty-one, she had never had a thought of writing a play, but was now hooked.

Lynne wrote three plays under the auspices of Miriam Colon and the Puerto Rican Travelling Theatre: *Graciela,* which was presented at the Puerto Rican Travelling Theatre; *Mundo,* which premiered at IATI Theatre Off-Broadway in 1983; the third play, *The Guitarron,* earned Lynne an NEA Fellowship and premiered in 1984 at St. Clements Theatre in New York.

Lynne was a member of New Dramatists for seven years where she wrote *Hidden Parts* (1981) which won the Kesselring Award in 1983. She also wrote *The Wonderful Tower of Humbert Lavoigent* (1983), which won two awards: The Le Compte De Nouey Award in 1984 and an FDG/CBS Award for Best Play and later, Best Production at Capital Repertory Company in Albany, New York in 1984/85. The same year, The Actors Theatre of Louisville commissioned a one-act play which became the full-length play, *Thin Air: Tales from a Revolution. Thin Air* premiered at the San Diego Repertory Company in 1987 and won a Drama League Award and a Rockefeller Fellowship in 1988. Lynne won a second NEA Fellowship in 1989/90. She has worked extensively with ACT and both its Conservatories which have premiered *The Reincarnation of Jaime Brown, Eddie Mundo Edmundo,* and *Analiese.*

Lynne has also done commissioned translations and adaptations: *The Damsel and the Gorilla* or *The Red Madonna* by Fernando Arrabal for INTAR in 1988 and Tirso de Molina's *Don Juan of Seville* for Classic Stage Company in 1990. Lynne's musical adaptations of the children's stories *Rikki-Tikki-Tavi* and *The Pied Piper of Hamlin* were produced by The Repertory Theatre of St. Louis in 1991 and 1992 respectively and her adaptation of …*And Now Miguel* was commissioned and premiered by the Lincoln Center Institute in 1995.

AUTHOR'S NOTE

Before I became obsessed with science fiction as a teenager, I loved fairy tales. I loved the drama, the splendor and the utter cruelty of them; the exotic imagery and magical love they expressed. I know I read every book of fairy tales on the large shelves of our local library. My favorite, and one that has haunted me, was "The Snow Queen" by Hans Christian Anderson. As a child it was because of the talking flowers and devils and ice palaces; later as a near-adult, it was because of its story of sexual awakening, and finally as I matured,

I loved it because I suspected it was the story of an older woman who falls in love with a young boy. This last insight was born out when I read Anderson's poem "The Snow Queen" which predated the story—and it told in less metaphorical terms as I had always sensed—of an older woman who spies a beautiful young boy with rosy cheeks and falls in love with him. So this was the crux of the story along with the glorious images and fantastic characters. Therefore it was natural to come back to this story when Craig Slaight, the Director of ACT's Young Conservatory came to me for a play that would appeal to all ages but would have protagonists who could be acted by young actors. *Analiese* is the result. It is a completely re-created tale. The characters and situations are quite different, although I continued to set the drama in Denmark. However, I moved the story forward to the end of the nineteenth century when Strindberg was first being performed in Sweden and Denmark since the "older woman" is now an actress. I only hope I have made a moving plausible drama that still has the intricacy and beauty of the fairy tale.

ORIGINAL PRODUCTION

Analiese was commissioned and first presented by the Young Conservatory New Plays Program at American Conservatory Theater (Carey Perloff, Artistic Director; Heather Kitchen, Managing Director), San Francisco, California, in July, 1997. It was directed by Craig Slaight; visual designs by Elizabeth Mead; costumes by Callie Floor; dance and movement by Chris Mattison; lighting by James Bock; the assistant director was Kevin Crook. The cast was as follows:

THE TOUCAN	Julia Mattison
ANALIESE	Danya Wachner Solomon
THE PEACOCK	Chase Oliver
CHRISTIAN	Mishi Schueller
NINA IVERSEN	Summer Serafin
HENNER	Kevin Crook
THE SERVING GIRL	Elizabeth Cole
JARL	Anna Hollenbach
PETER	Jeffrey Condeff
ERIK	Jeffrey Condeff
THE DANCERS	Anna Hollenbach
	Kevin Crook
THE GIRL	Elizabeth Cole
THE BOY	Chase Oliver

CHARACTERS

THE TOUCAN: Large tropical bird (can be played by a child)
ANALIESE: Girl 14–15 years old
PEACOCK: Tropical bird (non-speaking)
CHRISTIAN: Boy 16–17 years old
NINA IVERSEN: 30 year old Famous Actress
HENNER: Man (non-speaking)
SERVANT GIRL: (non-speaking)
JARL: Teenage boy
PETER: Teenage boy
ERIK: Teenage boy
YOUNG GIRL SPIRITUAL WARRIOR: 10 years old
YOUNG BOY SPIRITUAL WARRIOR: 10–11 years old
HANS: Spiritual Warrior Boy age 18
SIGRUN: Robber girl 17 years old
CARL: 20 year old Painter
DANCERS: Adult,(non-speaking)

TIME AND PLACE

All action takes place in Odense, the North Beach of Funen, and in the
northern regions of Jutland, Denmark, in 1898.

SCENE I

Stage is empty except for a wooden boat with oars center stage. Analiese is rowing with great effort facing the prow. A large Toucan sits on the stern. Analiese is not aware of the bird.

ANALIESE: *(Exhausted.)* Skagen. Skagen. I must reach Skagen. *(She rows more. Her hands hurt. She looks at her hands.)* Blood. *(She pulls the sleeves over her hands and keeps rowing.)* I must reach Skagen. *(Sings to herself breathing hard.)*
"The water is wide, I cannot cross over
And neither have I wings to fly..."
God help me.
Right hand, left hand, right hand, left hand, right hand, left...I can't do it. I can't. To have come so far...so far. It isn't fair. God on High, hear me... *(She stops completely winded and scans her surroundings. She sees the Toucan.)* What? I have lost my mind entirely. What are you doing here? I must be seeing things.
(She starts to rise to touch the Toucan to see if it's real, but the bird opens its wings and flaps as if it is about to fly off. Analiese sits down very slowly.)
ANALIESE: Don't leave.
(The bird sees that Analiese is staying put and settles itself down again.)
ANALIESE: How did you get here, you poor thing? Did you escape? Do you remember me? I saw you in the Aviary. You're a Toucan. You come from the jungle. It seems like years and years ago I saw you, but it was only months, wasn't it? Could it have been only months ago? That was the last time I saw Christian too. Oh Toucan, it's cold. What a mistake we've made. So far from home. This is no place to be free. *(Sadly.)* Christian. *(Angry, calling.)* Chriiiss-tiaan! Where are you when I need you? Christian! If only you hadn't met that horrid woman.

SCENE II

Analiese steps out of the boat. She is in an aviary in winter. Lots of light, bird calls and songs heard. A peacock struts on one wooden cube. A Toucan sits preening its feathers on another cube of a different height. Analiese is followed by Christian. They both carry heavy winter coats.

ANALIESE: Christian it's so hot. It's like summer. It's wonderful. Here! *(She hands Christian her coat.)* I knew it would be like this. Look—oh there's a peacock. Doesn't it looks like a prince? Doesn't he look like he has hundreds of eyes on his tail? *(She tries to pet it, but it scurries away. She goes to the peacock which cocks it's head at her. She copies his movements.)* Pretty boy. Pretty boy. Hello. Hello. *(The peacock goes to nip her and she jumps back.)* You mean old thing.

CHRISTIAN: *(Is over by the Toucan who regards him solemnly.)* Analiese. Come over here. Look at this bird. What a lordly fellow. I wonder what he is.

ANALIESE: His beak's bigger than his body. If he tried to fly he'd fall over on his face.

CHRISTIAN: I really don't think so, Analiese.

ANALIESE: I know that. I'm not such a child as you think. Christian—this is the best. I'm so glad you brought me.

CHRISTIAN: Just be glad your Grandmother's a good cook and I like to stay on her good side.

ANALIESE: You brought me because you like me.

CHRISTIAN: Who could like a scrawny little chicken like you?

ANALIESE: You used to beg me to marry you every two weeks.

CHRISTIAN: What was I, three years old?

ANALIESE: No. Six.

CHRISTIAN: Here take your coat. I've got my own to carry. *(He goes off to look at the other birds.)*

ANALIESE: You were nicer as a little boy, I'll tell you that.

(A fine lady in furs enters with a gentleman and a maid she hands her furs to without looking.)

NINA: *(Goes to the Toucan. Addresses the gentleman.)* Henner—that's a Toucan. Poor thing so far from home and caught in our endless Danish Winter. Do you miss the jungle my pretty one? Flying free in the tree tops with your monkey friends chattering about? *(To anyone who's listening.)* He's sacrificed so much to bring us beauty. It's almost like being an actress.

ANALIESE: But there's a difference, Ma'am.

NINA: Excuse me?

ANALIESE: *(Curtsies.)* The bird was captured. He had no choice whether he should bring us beauty or not.

NINA: Artists have no choice either, my dear. *(To Henner.)* Who is this girl? She's very bold.

(Analiese curtsies. Nina moves off. She appraises Christian. Two teenage friends rush in and surprise Christian. One punches him in the arm.)

CHRISTIAN: Hey!

JARL: So, you coming sledding or not? We've been waiting for hours.

PETER: You should have seen Jarl acting like an idiot.

JARL: I was not.

PETER: Stupid bugger almost got killed. Hitched his sled to a very dashing sleigh and was whipped under it's runners.

JARL: I planned that. The sleigh was damn fast and I skidded out again.

PETER: You planned that?! *(To Christian.)* So?

CHRISTIAN: Analiese...

ANALIESE: I can't believe you're leaving. Don't you want to see the birds?

PETER: Birds are for babies.

JARL: *(Poking him.)* I wouldn't be so quick to say that. Look who else is here.

PETER: God in Heaven. Isn't that Nina Iversen, the actress?

JARL: It's her or an angel.

ANALIESE: She is beautiful.

CHRISTIAN: Very.

JARL: They say the King was her lover.

CHRISTIAN: Not the King of Denmark?

JARL: No. Sweden. He wasn't the only one either. There were many.

PETER: Ooo-la-la, the things she must know.

JARL: We have to meet her. *(He takes a flower.)* I have just the thing. How do I look?

PETER: *(Grabs the flower and offers it to Christian.)* You're too ugly. Here, Christian. You give it to her. I dare you.

CHRISTIAN: Why don't you do it if you're so keen?

JARL: You look older. You're taller. Go on don't be a bloody coward.

PETER: Or will your little "wife" get mad?

CHRISTIAN: She's not my wife. *(He takes the flower and goes to Nina.)*

ANALIESE: I don't care. Go make a fool of yourself! *(Says to the Toucan.)* Boys are so stupid. If you tease them enough you can make them do anything. They'll jump off a cliff to prove what little men they are.

PETER: And what will girls do—cry?

(Analiese walks away. Now that Christian is next to Nina he is very nervous. Nina is facing away. He clears his throat and gives a little stiff bow.)

NINA: *(Turns towards him, but addresses Henner.)* Ah, the young man with the golden skin.

CHRISTIAN: You're Miss Nina Iversen, the actress?

NINA: I am. And you?

CHRISTIAN: *(Bowing again.)* Christian Pyndt, Ma'am.

NINA: And that flower you're clutching in your hand, might that be for me?

CHRISTIAN: How idiotic. *(He gives it to her.)* Yes of course it's for you.

NINA: A white rose. Mmmmmm, it's perfect. Look Henner, a white rose, wouldn't you know?

CHRISTIAN: What?

NINA: White roses are my favorite.

CHRISTIAN: No. You're making fun of me.

NINA: You're a lovely boy and this is a lovely gesture.

CHRISTIAN: Then I've offended you somehow.

NINA: No. You've brought back a rush of memories, that's all.

CHRISTIAN: Not very good ones I'm afraid. You don't seem pleased.

NINA: Now, I've made you feel badly. I am sorry. It's just—well I'll confide in you a little bit because you're so forward and so dear. *(She takes him by the arm and takes him aside.)* A gentleman I was very much in love with used to fill my rooms with white roses after every performance at the Royal Theater. You can't imagine how many he sent or how their fragrance used to float through my life in those days as if it were the air itself. I can't smell a white rose without thinking of him.

CHRISTIAN: I see. Then I must apologize.

NINA: Apologize? But why?

CHRISTIAN: One rose can hardly be worth your while.

NINA: No, no, no. I love the rose. I haven't had a single white rose since my friend left. So actually, yours is very precious.

(Christian is pleased and doesn't know where to look.)

NINA: You said your name was...

CHRISTIAN: Christian Pyndt, Ma'am.

NINA: Christian. Here's my card. And this is where I stay when I'm in town. Unfortunately, I'm leaving tonight or I would invite you up for tea.

CHRISTIAN: I should love to come for tea and you should tell me more about your life.

NINA: Yes, we should have a splendid talk. But I'm afraid I must go North.

CHRISTIAN: North? In Winter?

NINA: Yes as far North as I can—almost to Skagen. I have an estate. I call it the Ice Palace. It's so austere and white in Winter—so deserted. I love to feel the stripping down of conventional time. I love...oh you cannot guess how the living of this life any life involves great and private pain which we share with no one. But at the Ice Palace—the pain trails away. It's not so quiet there or so removed that you can't hear yourself think, or that you would even wish to—but you can hear your heart beat.

You're too young to have your store of pain yet. I hope you never do. What you would like are the falcons and the sea eagles and the polar bears and whales!

CHRISTIAN: Absolutely! I'd love to hunt a whale or a bear! Are there wolves?

NINA: Oh yes.

CHRISTIAN: You're so right to go North. No one else ever thinks of it.

NINA: I have an idea. What are you doing now?

CHRISTIAN: This afternoon?

NINA: Yes.

CHRISTIAN: I'm going sledding. Why?

NINA: You go with the boys in the square outside?

CHRISTIAN: Yes we hitch our sleds to the fastest ride. Why?

NINA: *(Looks at Henner and smiles.)* I think I'll bring my sleigh by so I can wave to you. I'll throw you a kiss and embarrass you in front of your friends. *(She laughs, takes Henner's arm and they exit.)*

CHRISTIAN: Oh God. I'll die.

(Peter and Jarl rush up.)

JARL: So? So?

PETER: I can't believe she talked to you that long! What did she say?

(Analiese comes up.)

CHRISTIAN: She gave me her card.

JARL: You fop.

CHRISTIAN: *(Looking at Analiese.)* She's leaving tonight. So I don't think she meant anything by it.

ANALIESE: Let's go. I want to go home.

CHRISTIAN: But you so wanted to come.

ANALIESE: It's only birds and flowers. I've seen those before.

PETER: Tell me every word she said to you.

CHRISTIAN: Analiese.

JARL: She touched your arm. Twice. You lucky dog.

PETER: I can smell her perfume on you.

ANALIESE: Your friends are beastly! They've spoiled everything.

CHRISTIAN: I'll get them away. We'll go sledding and I'll come back for you. Meet me under the clock. I'll only be gone an hour or so.

ANALIESE: Fine.

CHRISTIAN: Now don't cry. It makes your nose all red and ugly.

PETER: Come on, Chris.

JARL: Come on.

(They take him away.)

JARL: Peter's right you do smell like Miss Iversen. If I close my eyes I might kiss you.

CHRISTIAN: (*He looks at Analiese who is crying. He walks back and hands her his handkerchief.*) Here. I'm only going sledding and you've been pestering me for weeks to bring you here. So enjoy it.

PETER: Mr. Pyndt!

ANALIESE: I wish you were six again. (*She returns the handkerchief.*)

CHRISTIAN: Then you'd be only three. Aren't things much better now if you really think about it?

JARL: I can't stand such tender good-byes.

PETER: They make me sick. Come on or the square will be deserted.

CHRISTIAN: (*To Analiese.*) I must take care of these half-wits. They obviously can't do a thing without me.

JARL: Half-wits? You cretin.

CHRISTIAN: Nit-wits.

(*They leave.*)

SCENE III

Analiese has stopped rowing to rest. The Toucan is cawing. It stops its caw again.

ANALIESE: Oh I agree. I could have killed him. Did he really think I would wait like a good little lamb until he'd had his fun? I left right away. I had to walk. It was nearly dark too. An omnibus passed but I had no money and the horses kicked mud on my coat. I was furious. I never wanted to speak to him again! I cursed him and wished him dead a hundred times, leaving me like that! (*She starts to row and then stops.*) How was I to know he had already disappeared? All the time I cursed him, he was already gone. (*She pulls her sleeves down to cover her hands and rows.*) We found his sled the next morning on the river where the ice had broken up. I never saw him again. I had cursed him! What penance could I make that would be grievous enough-to punish me for my horrid thoughts? I forced myself to pass the river everyday where Christian had died. I put branches on the ice to mark the spot where he had fallen through and sat in this boat until I was so cold it hurt. No one ever came. The boat was abandoned too. There was even water frozen in the bottom. So I sat there every day waiting to see a hand appear or his glove, or his eyeless blue face pressing up suddenly under the ice.

(The Toucan cocks its head and looks at her first with one side and then the other. It searches the boat for food.)

ANALIESE: February, March, April the river woke. The ice was melting. One day I sat in the boat eating some bread and trying to picture Christian's face—but a fearsome angel flashed through my mind in white robes with wings that reached from his shoulders to the ground. His face was stern and grave and suddenly he swung a broad silver sword—I swear I could see the glint of it. Then a rush of water moved the boat. It began to drift.

(The Toucan rubs its beak with his wing.)

ANALIESE: Yes I should have jumped, but a strange calmness overtook me. I felt this certainty that I would join Christian—dead or alive. Two boys passed and yelled to me, but I couldn't hear them. The water in the bottom had melted and I found two oars. Soon the river spread out and brought me to a wide beach. There was the ocean. Fear had caught up with me and I was relieved to see the beach. I could find my way back to Odense. A big clumsy boy passed carrying two buckets of coal.

(The Toucan caws.)

ANALIESE: I am so thirsty.

SCENE IV

Analiese steps out of the boat and approaches the boy carrying coal.

ANALIESE: Excuse me. Could you tell me how I might get back to Odense?
(The boy continues walking and won't look at her, as if he is much younger and afraid.)

ANALIESE: I've done something very stupid and now I must get back. Please stop a moment.
(The boy looks off stage guiltily, puts one bucket down and then the other and stands waiting like an ox for his next instruction.)

ANALIESE: Can you tell me where I am?

ERIK: *(Looks at her as if she's crazy.)* The beach.

ANALIESE: I know. But what beach?

ERIK: *(Carefully picks up one bucket and then the other.)* I can take you to Jutland.

ANALIESE: That's across the bay.

ERIK: Grandpa Urs is a ferryboat man. When he dies I get his boat. He's not really my Grandpa. My father's head was cracked under a carriage wheel.

ANALIESE: I see.

ERIK: My mother didn't want me because I'm simple. Papa was a drunk. Grandpa Urs likes me cuz I'm his eyes now. He's old.

ANALIESE: Are you going to see Grandpa Urs now?

(Erik starts walking.)

ANALIESE: Can I go with you? Does he go to Odense?

ERIK: Sometimes. I think. He has his ferryboat sixty-eight years. I been going... *(He puts his buckets down and counts laboriously on his fingers.)* ...six. Wait. *(He stops again. Takes a small mound out of his pocket. Unwraps it, takes a very small bite out of something and chews it slowly.)* Chocolate.

ANALIESE: Grandpa Urs must be very good to you if he gives you chocolate.

ERIK: *(Looks at her as if she's crazy.)* The rich lady give it to me. If I eat one bite every day, I can make it last to... *(He hands the handkerchief with chocolate to Analiese.)* If I don't eat any...to *(Counts on his fingers.)* Next month. Six months.

ANALIESE: Oh, you got this six months ago?

ERIK: Five. November. Next month will be six. I can count pretty good. Next year I'll get more chocolate because I'm bigger and I can push the others away.

ANALIESE: Why would you push them? Why not just ask?

ERIK: No. Did you ever see a walrus? They smell just like a pig. One tried to tipple our boat. *(Taps his head.)* I threw some fish as far as I could from the boat and the walrus went away after it. Next year—when the lady throws chocolates from her boat—I'll grab some and throw them far away so the other boys go off after them—just like the walrus.

ANALIESE: That's very smart.

ERIK: *(He gives her a big smile.)* Yeah. Give me back my chocolate. *(He takes it.)* In November I go to Odense with Grandpa Urs and the lady with red hair throws chocolates from her boat. She's rich. She doesn't use our boat of course. She goes to...to...Skagen.

ANALIESE: How do you know she goes to Skagen? Did she tell you?

ERIK: I didn't talk to her! *(Looks at her like she's crazy.)* I don't know the woman. I talked to the boy with her. He ran to the boat and knocked me down, then picked me up and cleaned my face. He said they were going to Skagen. He was tall. He gave me his handkerchief. See, I got my chocolate in it. *(He unwraps his chocolate and hands her the handkerchief.)*

ANALIESE: You say the boy went to Skagen? With a woman?

ERIK: Grandpa Urs say she's a woman and then some. He says her hair is the color of the Danish flag.

ANALIESE: Red?

ERIK: Sure. He said he'd salute her anytime.

ANALIESE: The boy was alive?

ERIK: *(Rolls his eyes and sighs.)* Of course.

ANALIESE: Tell me…

ERIK: How could he give me the handkerchief if he was dead?

ANALIESE: Does your Grandpa Urs take his boat to Skagen?

ERIK: We go to Jutland. To…to Glatvid Strand for the seals. The sea's too big at Skagen. Maybe if you had a lot of money Grandpa Urs would make a special trip.

ANALIESE: I have no money.

(Erik stops and puts his buckets down.)

ERIK: Then Grandpa Urs won't take you anywhere.

ANALIESE: Could you help me? Could you sneak me on board?

ERIK: *(Agitated.)* I don't know. Sometimes he hits me. I'm bigger but I let him. I scream too.

ANALIESE: You could hide me.

ERIK: I don't know…

ANALIESE: Like a game. Hide and seek. I would hide where Grandpa Urs would never find me.

ERIK: Sure. But I couldn't hide. I have to work. *(Whispers to her.)* Sometimes I hide.

ANALIESE: Yes?

ERIK: I hide in the coal bin. You could hide there too.

ANALIESE: I suppose so.

ERIK: He never goes there. And you know what else? Here. *(He hand her his buckets.)* You can carry the buckets and I'll walk next to you. Grandpa Urs will think it's just me alone. His eyes are bad.

(Analiese starts back toward her boat.)

ERIK: Are you stupid? Where are you going? Grandpa Urs's boat is over this way.

ANALIESE: I must bring my boat and find a way to tie it to the ferry.

ERIK: I'll do that. I'm much stronger than you. I'll tell Grandpa Urs I found the boat and I want it to play in.

ANALIESE: *(Struggling with the buckets.)* Thank you. Thank you kind sir.

ERIK: *(Looks around frantically.)* Sir? Where?

ANALIESE: You. I called you sir.

ERIK: Me? Sir?

ANALIESE: Yes. You've acted like a gentleman. I cannot thank you enough.

ERIK: *(Straightens up.)* My name is Erik. Erik Blid.

(They exit.)

SCENE V

Nina's ball. There is only a screen that separates the ballroom from the balcony. Behind the screen we intermittently see couples dancing. We hear music faintly. Christian is out on the balcony in dress clothes.

NINA: Christian, what are you doing out here? Don't you like the music and the dancing?

CHRISTIAN: I think I saw a whale.

NINA: Where? Show me.

CHRISTIAN: There in the bay. Could it have been?

NINA: Yes. Sometimes gray whales wander in to feed.

CHRISTIAN: It was as big as a barn...or a ship!

NINA: You didn't answer my question. Do you hate the dance?

CHRISTIAN: I like it better out here.

NINA: Aren't you cold?

CHRISTIAN: Not at all. I could stay out here forever. Miss Iversen...Nina. I feel there's no limits with you. The world is endless. For all I know there's twice as many stars in the sky.

NINA: That's delightful.

CHRISTIAN: What?

NINA: That you love it here.

CHRISTIAN: I do. There is so much out there I know nothing about.

NINA: And it may be there is much in there *(She points inside.)* that you know nothing about.

CHRISTIAN: Oh. Have I done something stupid? Is everyone talking?

NINA: Would you care?

CHRISTIAN: I want to please you.

NINA: You do.

CHRISTIAN: We did say we'd be great friends.

NINA: We did. And I would be remiss in not pointing out that one does not leave one's friends in the lurch during social occasions. It seems I need a dance partner.

CHRISTIAN: There's at least five men dying to dance with you. Even I could see that.

NINA: Is that why you left?

CHRISTIAN: They have so much more to say to you than I do.

NINA: They certainly think so.

CHRISTIAN: Don't talk down to me. They do. Any wretch can see that. One is a famous surgeon and the other has painted half a dozen naked ladies from Stockholm to Pra ue—as he continually likes to mention.

NINA: *(Brushing back his)* Christian—what is it?

CHRISTIAN: I think you're most beautiful woman I've ever seen. There! Do I sound like every other man you've ever met?

NINA: No.

CHRISTIAN: Of course not.

NINA: The men I've met have said it hundreds of times to hundreds of women. I doubt you've ever said it before.

CHRISTIAN: *(Can't look at her.)* Do you think you could arrange for me to go whaling? I want to hunt whales.

NINA: You're such a boy.

CHRISTIAN: Why? Don't ladies want to go and have adventures too? Don't they like to master something, conquer something?

NINA: Yes some of us ladies do, but we don't often want to kill it. And why whales? I adore whales. They lead such obscure and exemplary lives— quite unlike…. actresses. And they speak. Did you know? Their voices sound like wind in a cave.

CHRISTIAN: It would please me to go.

NINA: I could arrange it. But it's very brutal. You'd be gone an awfully long time. I would miss you.

CHRISTIAN: At least I wouldn't be leaving here like a thief.

NINA: Ahhhhhh. That's what it is. You're homesick.

CHRISTIAN: I'm not proud of how I left. I stole away like a thief. Poor Analiese must think I'm dead. How could I have done that?

NINA: You did what you had to do at the time. I've found that if you want to make your way in the world, you must be as pitiless as nature. She'll fascinate you one moment, coloring the cliffs black with auks in May and

June and then starve half a million to death in August. Sometimes it's for the best.

CHRISTIAN: I hope you're right.

NINA: I'll tell you what. Come dance with me and I'll make sure you become a great hunter. You can track polar bears and wolves and catch all the auks you like and press their little hearts until they die.

CHRISTIAN: You know many hunters then.

NINA: Yes many. Now indulge me. Let's see what your dance master has taught you.

SCENE VI

Analiese has gotten out of the boat and is pulling it onto a beach. We hear a stream. The Toucan sits on the prow looking all around. Woods sounds.

ANALIESE: A stream. *(She starts towards it.)* Look. There's a deer. Oh, one antler's broken off in a fight. *(She watches the deer leave, which we don't see.)* I wish he weren't afraid of me. But he's wiser than I have been.
(The Toucan drinks from the stream. Scoops up the water and lifts his head so it slides down his beak into his gullet.)

ANALIESE: *(To the Toucan.)* He's wiser than you too. Trusting strangers. Each person I met I thought was my savior. That was before I learned more about human nature; that you can't rely on people not to feel deeply; or flee or go mad...

SCENE VII

As Analiese says the last lines she tugs at the boat. A young girl runs in wildly and begins to spin in circles.

ANALIESE: Girl. Girl. Come help me with this boat.

GIRL: *(Twirling.)* I can't. I'm a lily. I'm a lily. I'm a tiger lily. *(She growls and falls to the ground.)*

ANALIESE: You're spoiled that's what you are.
(The girl doesn't get up. Analiese goes over to her.)

ANALIESE: Girl, are you all right?

GIRL: Listen to the drum—boom, boom!

ANALIESE: Look at you half naked and there's still snow on the ground. Who let you out like this?

(The girl moans.)

ANALIESE: Are you all right? Should I call your mother?

GIRL: There are only two notes—boom, boom. Hark—the women's dirge. Hark—the cry of priests. The Hindu woman stands on the funeral pyre in her long red robe; the flames fly up around her and her dead husband. But the Hindu woman is thinking of the living man there in the crowd whose eyes burn hotter than the flames that will soon burn her body to ashes.

ANALIESE: You're delirious. Where do you live? What can I do?

(A young boy stumbles in and sits suddenly staring vacantly.)

ANALIESE: Boy! You there! *(She starts towards him.)*

GIRL: Hot! Can the heart's flame perish in the flames of the pyre?

(Analiese goes back to the girl afraid to leave her.)

ANALIESE: You there, boy. Can you help me get this girl home?

(The girl falls asleep.)

ANALIESE: Wake up. You can't sleep. If you sleep in the snow, you'll die! *(She goes to the boy.)* Boy! Boy!

BOY: Leave me alone. *(He sleeps also.)*

ANALIESE: No. Wake up! What is the matter with you two? Are you poisoned?

BOY: I only speak my own story. I am a stork.

ANALIESE: You are mad.

BOY: *(Grasps her wrist suddenly.)* I know the pond where all little human babies lie till the storks fetch them and give them to their parents. Now we shall fly to the pond and fetch a little brother for the boy who threw stones at us.

ANALIESE: Yes of course we shall. *(She looks around desperately for help.)*

BOY: Yes.

ANALIESE: But if the boy threw stones and was bad and wicked—why bring him a baby? Why don't I take you home?

BOY: In the pond is a little dead baby—it has dreamed itself to death. We'll take it to the boy and he'll cry because we have brought him a little dead brother.

(Hans, an older boy runs in.)

HANS: There you are you wicked children. How many times do I have to tell you not to open that…Who are you?

ANALIESE: *(Struggling to get up and curtsy.)* My name's Analiese and…

HANS: Don't bother curtseying. We don't do that here.

ANALIESE: What do you do here? Poison children?

HANS: There's no time to explain. Give me a hand with the girl. I'll take the boy. Follow me.

(They carry the children across the stage.)

ANALIESE: What is your name?

HANS: Hans.

ANALIESE: What's wrong with the children?

HANS: They've been naughty.

ANALIESE: I see.

HANS: But you don't. I'm responsible for them and now I'll be in a lot of trouble.

ANALIESE: Is that all you can think about?

HANS: They'll be all right. This isn't the first time they've gotten into the cookie jar. Here we are. *(Hans lays the boy down and motions for Analiese to do the same with the girl.)* They'll sleep it off.

ANALIESE: What? Cookies?

HANS: Hardly. *(He straightens his clothing and bows.)* Well hello. Thank you for your help.

ANALIESE: May I sit down?

HANS: Yes certainly.

ANALIESE: Is there something to drink? I'm dying of thirst.

HANS: There's cold tea. *(Fetches her a jar.)*

(Analiese gulps it down.)

HANS: You're awfully brown. Aren't ladies still fashionably pale? It's been some time since I've moved in social circles you could say. Actually, you look quite burned. Does it hurt?

ANALIESE: Yes a bit.

HANS: The Elders say cold tea will take away the sting. Just a minute. *(He fetches a rag soaked in tea.)*

ANALIESE: I'm sorry to be such trouble.

HANS: No trouble. Would you like me to...

ANALIESE: No. I'll do it. Thank you. *(She takes the rag and presses it to her face, neck and arms.)*

HANS: Did you have a shipwreck? Did the rest of your party die?

ANALIESE: *(Shocked.)* No! Why do you ask?

HANS: You seem to be alone. And if you'll pardon me for saying this. You seem to be in terrible condition. All bones and hair.

ANALIESE: I'll be fine in a moment. Thank you.

HANS: There's some dried fish if you like.

ANALIESE: More tea please. I won't bother you much longer.

HANS: *(Brings water and watches her closely as she gulps it down.)* You really must stay with us and rest. It will be quite proper. The Elders will be here any minute. I'm sure they'll help you get back to wherever you've come from.

ANALIESE: No thank you. There's someone waiting for me up ahead. He'll be very worried if I don't make it.

HANS: I see. Where is your meeting place?

ANALIESE: Oh. Up near Skagen.

HANS: That's a long ways. Come. You must stay with us. You don't have much strength and you can hardly walk there alone. It's several days journey and although most of the animals you meet seem charming—they're not when you get to know them. Especially wolves. I'd hate to meet one face to face. They're fascinating and they look at you like people do. But not good people.

ANALIESE: Wolves?

HANS: Yes. Even the deer will stomp you. Especially if you find one with a baby.

ANALIESE: I wouldn't walk anyway. I have a boat. I'll go along the coast. It's quite serene.

HANS: You don't look very presentable for a meeting.

ANALIESE: Oh yes. The coal bin. I'm filthy.

HANS: You seem to have ripped your dress in several places.

ANALIESE: Where?

HANS: *(Touching her lightly, but they are both very aware of it.)* Here and over here. You must get cold.

ANALIESE: Yes I do.

HANS: We're great weavers here. I know we'll have something to cover it with. *(He exits and comes back with a large homespun brown shawl.)* It's a pity, everything we make is brown.
(Again he helps her on with the shawl and they are very aware of each other physically.)

ANALIESE: I really can't keep this...

HANS: Please don't refuse out of any stupid convention of propriety. I detest that. Propriety's one of the few things I'm glad we left behind.

ANALIESE: By "we"—you mean your family?

HANS: Of sorts. "We" are a spiritual community. There's twenty-two of us. All adults except for the wee ones and I. We consider ourselves spiritual warriors foraging for a pure life in the woods. We call ourselves the New Vikings—although we're not the "let's heave rocks and eat brains" variety. And no human sacrifices. Just the occasional bird or horse. In fact, the Elders are down by the river offering horse entrails to Loki, as we speak. Loki is a very tricky fellow and deserves only the best.

ANALIESE: I'm afraid I don't know who Loki is.

HANS: You're a Christian I suppose.

ANALIESE: Yes certainly.

HANS: We were too once. However, now we're true Northmen. We worship the old gods—you must have heard of Thor or Odin, who hung for nine nights from the Tree of the World until he could see the future. Loki is the river god. He acts up in the Spring.

ANALIESE: You don't believe in one God?

HANS: The White Christ? Hardly. We're animists with some modern adjustments. You must want to eat now. There's some cold soup I made. I am a good cook, but a dreadful hunter.

ANALIESE: I've imposed enough.

HANS: Didn't I tell you. False modesty is pointless. *(He gets some soup.)* I seem to have a terrible headache. Excuse me. *(He takes two tablets out of his pouch and swallows them quickly.)*

ANALIESE: Aren't you afraid you'll go to Hell if you're not a Christian?

HANS: No we've found something more majestic. We've bridged the idea that on the one hand, God took some dirt and shaped us in his image—you do know that as a Christian no matter how good looking you are—and I find you reasonably attractive—you're nothing but glorified dirt. And on the other hand God breathed life into you so the essence of God is in you. That was two halves that didn't fit. How can you be dirt *and* God? The Vikings were right in the first place. You can be dirt and God if God *is* everything—the white birch, the squirrel, the poplar, the sun, the river. To us the whole natural world is sacred.

ANALIESE: I like the way you talk.

HANS: How do I talk?

ANALIESE: Beautiful and complicated.

HANS: Really? I haven't had much practice. It's all been in my head.

ANALIESE: You should be a poet.

HANS: Thank you. That's very kind. I hope to be one. I've read so many poets. I read a tremendous amount. The Elders brought books with them. Hundreds. But I think I've read them all four times by now. My head is full of useful topics—Hindu rituals, the discovery of Africa, the proper construction of meat-drying racks. I read to the children to keep from going mad.

ANALIESE: The children! I'd nearly forgot. You must be worried about them.

(Hans checks.)

ANALIESE: Are they your brother and sister?

HANS: No. No relation.

ANALIESE: And there's no one else near your age?

HANS: No such luck. So actually it's quite nice we stumbled into each other.

ANALIESE: Yes it is. I think you saved my life.

HANS: What kind of person let you travel alone in such dangerous circumstances?

ANALIESE: No one let me. I chose to.

HANS: You ran away.

(Analiese doesn't answer.)

HANS: Let me guess—a young man is involved in this.

ANALIESE: Yes.

HANS: And he's waiting breathlessly for your arrival?

ANALIESE: Yes. Near Skagen, I believe.

HANS: "I believe"? So you're not sure. That means he isn't waiting for you. Is he even expecting you?

ANALIESE: It doesn't matter. I must see if he's there. He might have passed this way last November. You might even have seen him. He was traveling with his...aunt. She has red hair and is very rich.

HANS: His Aunt? And her name?

ANALIESE: You wouldn't know it.

HANS: If they pass regularly I might. We trade with travelers all the time.

ANALIESE: It's not important.

HANS: I see. And you're not worried because this young man...

ANALIESE: Christian.

HANS: How fitting. So. You're not worried that Christian's been alone with his red-haired Aunt all winter?

ANALIESE: Certainly not.

HANS: Is she ugly then?

ANALIESE: No quite beautiful

HANS: I see.

ANALIESE: Would you stop saying "I see." You don't believe a word I've said.

HANS: There's no sense in worrying. Looks aren't everything. We all have our value. As a friend of mine once said "If only the most beautiful birds could sing, all the woods would be a silent place indeed."

ANALIESE: That's pretty but not very complimentary to me. Will the Elders be here soon?

HANS: I think you need more tea. I'll put a couple of my tablets in it. They're good for what ails you.

ANALIESE: What are they?

HANS: A flower extract. Opium. The British bring it from India. It's quite nice. I've taken some and my head has stopped throbbing. *(Counts them out.)* One, two. That should be enough the first time.

ANALIESE: *(Takes them.)* Thank you.

HANS: It may be a little bitter. I wouldn't mention this to the Elders though. I mean, the pills are harmless. They give you the most amazing dreams. I saw death once. He was a strong old man with a scythe in his hand and great black wings. He was quite friendly. Since then I've lost all fear of death.

ANALIESE: I don't like that you're asking me to lie.

HANS: Not lie. Just keep something back. I can't believe you tell everyone everything that goes on in your life. Otherwise you wouldn't be here.

ANALIESE: You're right.

HANS: Only the Elders are supposed to take these during ceremonies. But I see them sneak a few now and then. They can be quite powerful when you take a lot. We use them to contact our spiritual guides from the past. The Vikings appear to us in dreams and explain their myths.

ANALIESE: Could I have more tea. But no pills.

HANS: Certainly. *(He puts more pills in her tea.)* You seem like such a nice person. It's good to talk to you. However, I have something unpleasant to say. Here's more tea.

ANALIESE: What?

HANS: How to tell you this.

ANALIESE: Just say it!

HANS: A party did come through these woods last November. We were surprised anyone was traveling north at that time. There were two carriages. One had a very lovely red-haired woman traveling with a young man. He had light hair and that golden kind of skin. I remember thinking he was probably a Swede.

ANALIESE: Yes. Yes go on.

HANS: They had a beautiful fur robe thrown over their laps. But then…the wheel on one of the carriages broke as they went over a stream and they were killed.

ANALIESE: It can't be. You're mistaken.

HANS: I'm truly sorry. That's how we got the horses for the sacrifice.

ANALIESE: Oh no! No.

HANS: I am sorry.

ANALIESE: Where are they buried? Take me to see them.

HANS: I'm afraid there was quite a current and they washed out to sea.

ANALIESE: Oh no. Not Christian. Surely not him.

HANS: *(Tries to comfort her awkwardly.)* So you see. You really must stay.

ANALIESE: My beautiful boy.

HANS: There. There. All isn't lost.

ANALIESE: But it is.

HANS: You think so. But you're so young. You could...you can bring so much goodness to the world still.

ANALIESE: I can't think of that.

HANS: So much loveliness. Analiese.

ANALIESE: Hans, please.

HANS: One door is closed, but another opens.

ANALIESE: I must find him.

HANS: If you searched all the beaches of Denmark, how could you possibly find him? If you found anything at all it would only be bones or worse and unrecognizable. Stay here, Analiese. I would be good to you. I would help you through this terrible time and you could save me.

ANALIESE: Hans I hardly know you.

HANS: *(Kneels suddenly and takes her hand.)* Save me.

ANALIESE: Hans, how can I save you?

HANS: Please.

ANALIESE: Save you from what?

HANS: I will dream myself to death. Analiese please. I need your help. I think I'm getting worse. I gave the children opium to keep them quiet while I was dreaming—such gorgeous dreams of color and music. They almost make it bearable here. But I gave the children opium! I gave them too much and they wondered off. What if they had fallen asleep and a wild animal tore them apart? What if they walked into the water and drowned? The worst is I think I would do anything to anyone to keep dreaming. Analiese, stay please. You can have a good life here. You can keep me from harming anyone.

ANALIESE: Could I?

HANS: Yes.

ANALIESE: But Hans, you gave me opium. You said it was harmless.

HANS: I won't do it again. I swear on a thousand stallions, on Thor, on the White Christ if you like. I didn't know how to make you stay, and I needed you to see how seductive it is. How sweet your nerves become, like spun sugar.

ANALIESE: *(Stands up abruptly.)* I must go.

HANS: You can't. It's dangerous.

ANALIESE: Why?

HANS: I …gave you more than you think. Two more pills. Sit down. You must. We can talk tomorrow. It will be clearer tomorrow.
(Analiese sits.)

HANS: Good. Good. Everything will be all right.
(One of the children moans and thrashes about.)

ANALIESE: Hans. Go to the children.

HANS: You will consider it?

ANALIESE: The children need you. The Elders will be back soon.

HANS: Yes. Yes, of course. *(He goes to them.)*
(Analiese bolts out of the door and runs some distance. She stops to catch her breath.)

ANALIESE: Oh God, Christian can you really be dead? *(She sits down shakily. She falls asleep.)*

SCENE VIII

Christian and Nina. She is reciting lines to him from "Miss Julie" and he is reading another part from a book.

NINA: You read that very well. Let's go on to the next. *(She turns the pages for him.)* I can't tell you how much help this has been. I'm extremely nervous about this role. We haven't seen a "Miss Julie" for nine years. I must make it mine. She must be imperious yet vulnerable.

CHRISTIAN: You must be a wonderful actress. I get so caught up with you that I lose my place.

NINA: I wish I could believe you, but you've never been to theater. All right, you're reading Jean, the servant. His girlfriend is asleep in the other room.

CHRISTIAN: We're here?

NINA: Yes, I shall begin. *(As Miss Julie.)* "A charming wife she'll make. Does she snore too?"

HANS: *(As Jean.)* "She doesn't do that, but she talks in her sleep."

NINA: *(Puts down the script.)* How does Jean know Christine talks in her sleep?

CHRISTIAN: He's heard her.

NINA: So you know what is going on there don't you?

CHRISTIAN: What?

NINA: Here where it says they look at each other. There is an understanding between them.

CHRISTIAN: Yes, that he sleeps with her.

NINA: Ah, so you know all about that sort of thing?

CHRISTIAN: Only what I've heard.

(They look at each other.)

NINA: Let's go on then from the look. *(As Miss Julie.)* Why don't you sit?

CHRISTIAN: *(As Jean.)* I wouldn't permit myself to do that in your presence.

NINA: *(As Miss Julie.)* But if I order you to?

CHRISTIAN: *(As Jean.)* Then I shall obey.

NINA: *(Miss Julie.)* Sit then. No, wait. Can you give me something to drink first?

CHRISTIAN: *(Jean.)* I don't know what we have in the ice-box. Only beer, I think.

NINA: *(Miss Julie.)* What do you mean, only beer? My taste is very simple. I prefer beer to wine. *(As Nina.)* Try to do the actions as they're written. Hand me a beer.

(Christian mimes giving her a beer.)

NINA: *(As Miss Julie.)* Thank you, won't you have some yourself?

CHRISTIAN: *(Jean.)* I'm not much of a drinker, but if madam orders me—

NINA: *(Miss Julie.)* Orders? Surely you know that a gentleman should never allow a lady to drink alone.

CHRISTIAN: *(Jean.)* That's perfectly true. *(Christian mimes opening a beer.)*

NINA: *(Miss Julie.)* Drink my health now! *(As Nina.)* Hesitate a minute. There. *(As Miss Julie.)* Are you shy?

CHRISTIAN: *(Jean.)* To my mistress's health!

NINA: *(Miss Julie.)* Bravo! Now kiss my shoe and the ceremony is complete.

(Christian starts to do so then pulls back.)

NINA: *(As Nina.)* Christian, do as it says.

(Christian looks at her then removes her shoe and brings his lips to her foot and kisses it lingeringly. He raises his head and looks at her.)

NINA: Christian, that's not...

CHRISTIAN: I know.

NINA: *(Withdraws her foot slowly.)* You've quite gotten into the role.

CHRISTIAN: The role is me, I think and you.

NINA: You're hardly a servant.

CHRISTIAN: But you're playing with me in all sorts of ways and I understand them all. *(He stands and moves close to her putting his arms around her.)* Just like in the play.

NINA: If things are to change. I must talk to you.

CHRISTIAN: I don't want to talk.

NINA: But you will. Sit.

CHRISTIAN: Am I Jean then? Is that an order?

NINA: Forget the play this is real life and I'm too fond of you to hurt you so we must understand each other.

CHRISTIAN: I told you I understand. You bring a young man here every winter and you "educate" him and then desert him. I've heard the servants and the whispers. Do you think that because I'm young I'm stupid?

NINA: No, but that's a harsh way of putting it. It makes both of us cheap and that is far from true—especially for you.

CHRISTIAN: You say that to all the boys.

NINA: No. To none of them. *(She brushes back her hair.)* I care about you. How do you feel about me?

CHRISTIAN: I can't express it.

NINA: You can do better than that. Tell me what you feel.

CHRISTIAN: You first. Do you feel anything for me?

NINA: I told you I did.

CHRISTIAN: Well what do you think when I'm in the room like this?

NINA: I think...I think your hair is so thick it's like broom bristles. *(She grasps his hair.)* I think that if I buried my fingers in it, it would be like grabbing a horse's mane. Now you. What do you think? What do you feel?

CHRISTIAN: I feel like a wheel of fire is rolling through my chest.

(Nina pulls away.)

NINA: Don't say wild things like that—you could make me fall in love with you.

CHRISTIAN: As much as you were with the man with the roses?

(Nina is silent.)

CHRISTIAN: Was that the King?

NINA: Is that what you've heard?

CHRISTIAN: Yes.

NINA: Don't believe everything you hear, Christian. It was not a great love affair on his part. You may be only seventeen, but it's time you learned some manners. You never, never mention a lady's...other interests unless she brings it up.

CHRISTIAN: You loved him. You're angry.

NINA: I should send you back home. You can sit under your cuckoo clock with your mother and father and eat meatballs and gravy.

CHRISTIAN: No!

NINA: Now your pouting.

CHRISTIAN: Just don't mention home.

NINA: The mood's spoiled for you, isn't it? But it will come back. Trust me. I'm a romantic idealist, you see. Don't be surprised. I believe with each new lover, I can reinvent myself and dispose of the troublesome person I've become—just like a snake shedding it's skin.

CHRISTIAN: I need some air.

NINA: Go on leave. I'm cross as well.

(Christian exits.)

SCENE IX

Analiese in the boat with the Toucan. There is thunder. The Toucan is unsettled and calls out and opens and closes its wings.

ANALIESE: Did you hear that sound? Is it thunder? I hear thunder but there's not a cloud in the sky. *(She listens.)* Thor is the God of Thunder, isn't he? I wonder if Hans is praying to him somewhere. I wonder if it does him any good. He should repulse me. How cruel to put opium in my tea. I had terrible nightmares. In one Christian and I were children again, making peepholes in the frosted windows with heated pennies we pressed against the glass. There was a great snowstorm—the snow fell faster and faster and the flakes were enormous. One became a woman dressed in white lace made up of millions of tiny star-shaped flakes that cut when you touched them. She was so pretty. She was made of ice but she was alive! Her eyes glittered. There was no peace in them. She nodded to us. Christian was wild to open the window. I couldn't stop him and he went out. When he turned to wave, his nose and fingers were black with cold. Does that mean he's really dead? Oh I should hate Hans, but I can't.

(Thunder again. The Toucan flaps its wings.)

ANALIESE: You heard it too. Thunder. It's the end of the world and we'll fall off and be ground to dust. No! I can't think like that. I mustn't give up. You never know what's next. Didn't that robber girl appear out of nowhere just when I thought I'd die? *(She steps out of the boat and lies face down.)*

SCENE X

A lone figure dragging a large bundle makes its way laboriously to where Analiese has collapsed. Sigrun sniffs around.

SIGRUN: *(Sniffing.)* Flowers! No! *(Sigrun opens her pack and pulls out two sticks of wood. Crosses them and then reacts as if it has become a lighted fire. She sighs, takes off her jacket, warms her hands and her butt. She sits and pulls out a long silver knife from her pack and then something to eat. She eats but sniffs again.)* Yep. Smell. Like flowers. *(She wets her finger and then wets each nostril and sniffs more avidly. She looks around in the snow and comes across Analiese.)* Hey, you! *(She squats looking at Analiese from head to toe. Lifts her head by her hair and lets it drop.)* Still soft. It looks like I shall have a playmate. *(She goes to her pack and takes out a blanket and wraps Analiese in it and gets her in a sitting position. She takes her knife and tests it on her finger.)* Ooooo! Good. Best knife. Poor Russians. *(She watches Analiese for a moment. Analiese is still asleep.)* Look, her little paws are twitching like a dog's when he's dreaming. *(She tickles Analiese's chin with her knife.)* Girl…oh girl. *(Sigrun goes through Analiese's pockets and finds nothing. She shakes her.)* Hey!

ANALIESE: Hans! Don't touch me! Get away!

SIGRUN: Well have it your own way.

ANALIESE: Oh God. *(She looks around wildly.)* Are you the only one here?

SIGRUN: Yep.

ANALIESE: Who are you?

SIGRUN: No name for you. Only my friends know my name. Don't tell me your name either. Knowing strangers names makes me sad. What if I have to kill you and you have a name. Like killing a pet. Too sad.
(Analiese is shaking violently, recovering from the cold. Sigrun goes in her pack and pulls out some raw meat and sticks it on the end of her knife.)

SIGRUN: You need food. *(She holds the meat over the two sticks as if cooking.)*

ANALIESE: What is that?

SIGRUN: Stag liver. Lucky I gutted a deer this morning. So, are you one of those Viking people? *(She laughs heartily.)*

ANALIESE: Why are you laughing?

SIGRUN: Tell me first. You one of them?

ANALIESE: No. You know them?

SIGRUN: Yep. Sure. I trade with them. *(She holds up her knife.)* I trade them their life for anything they're carrying. But they don't carry much—so I hardly bother them. Ummmmm—maybe sometimes for fun; when they do their ceremonies. *(She laughs again.)* Big, strong Vikings! They dream they're great warriors, but they only sit. They live in their heads. Puh! *(She spits.)* You sure you're not one of them?

ANALIESE: They gave me these clothes. But I'm not carrying anything.

SIGRUN: I know. *(Holds out meat.)* Here.

ANALIESE: No!…thank you.

SIGRUN: Fresh kill.

ANALIESE: No.

SIGRUN: What? You never eat meat?

ANALIESE: Yes, but…

SIGRUN: You don't think about where it comes from. From an animal. Nothing fancy. We're nothing fancy either. *(Sigrun belches.)*
(She eats and Analiese watches hungrily.)

ANALIESE: Maybe I'll have some.
(Sigrun gives her some and laughs heartily. Hans enters wrapped in a blanket. Analiese jumps up afraid.)

ANALIESE: Hans!

SIGRUN: So this is who you were afraid of? Hello Viking boy.

HANS: Don't interfere. I've handled you before.

SIGRUN: Then you were three. Now you're alone.

HANS: *(To Analiese.)* I must talk to you. I must apologize.

SIGRUN: *(To Analiese.)* So?

ANALIESE: Go away Hans. I have nothing to say to you.

HANS: You must let me explain.

SIGRUN: Give me your blanket and you can talk to the girl.
(Hans shoves it at Sigrun.)

SIGRUN: Nice blanket. *(She lays it on the ground and sits watching the two of them as if it were a cock fight.)*

ANALIESE: You could have killed me. Just like the children.

HANS: I never would have left you. I was coming for you. The Elders arrived. I had to wait. Did you see things?

ANALIESE: Bad things.

HANS: You see the power it has? You could lead me away from it, Analiese. I see that power and more in you.

ANALIESE: If I do have that power, it's one I never wanted and one I don't understand.
(Hans approaches. Analiese backs away. Sigrun is enjoying this.)

HANS: Don't back away. I stopped. See? I would never harm you. But that boy you love. He didn't deserve you. Look how much he's made you suffer; forcing you to travel alone and unprotected through a wilderness.

ANALIESE: He didn't force me. I already told you. I chose to.

HANS: I don't believe you. Love doesn't choose. It happens. It has happened to me.

ANALIESE: Hans.

HANS: With you. You see? You've made me a poet. I wrote you a poem. It's my first. *(He is trembling with cold and emotion.)* "I loved once but not again. Blindly, sullenly completely. I loved a girl not yet a woman. Green eyed as drunk as I was with golden skin and arms that smelled of woods and grass and ached for something as liquid and eternal as love…"

ANALIESE: Hans, just go back to your home. You frighten me.

HANS: Is that all you can say, Analiese?

SIGRUN: Ahhhh. Now I know your name. Analiese.

ANALIESE: Save the poem. It's wonderful. But give it to someone who can love you back. I never can.

HANS: *(To Sigrun.)* She thinks she's in love with a dead man. But I know better. *(To Analiese.)* I know you have deep feelings for me. *(He tries to embrace her.)*

(Sigrun steps in.)

SIGRUN: Are you deaf or crazy? She said she didn't want you.

(Hans looks at her knife, weighing whether he should fight Sigrun or not. He resigns himself to the moment.)

HANS: *(To Analiese.)* This girl is not your friend.

SIGRUN: Yes I am. I've decided. So Analiese, my name is Sigrun. Shall I let him go or kill him.

ANALIESE: Don't harm him. He'll leave. *(To Hans.)* If you love me as you say you do, you will leave.

HANS: All right. *(Backing away.)* You see? I'm gone. I've passed your first test. *(As he is leaving.)* I will see you again, Analiese. *(He exits.)*

ANALIESE: Thank you.

SIGRUN: Sigrun.

ANALIESE: Sigrun.

SIGRUN: So now you know my name.

ANALIESE: I won't forget it.

SIGRUN: But you're leaving?

ANALIESE: Yes.

SIGRUN: After a dead boy?

ANALIESE: I must.

SIGRUN: You have no horse.

ANALIESE: I have a boat.

SIGRUN: So! You should come with me. I'll get you good Russian boots. We'll go rob the Finns. We could become rich. I can show you sights you never dreamed. Bones of Whales and polar bears that lie about like the legs and arms of giants!

ANALIESE: I have my own way to go.

SIGRUN: Yep, well, as you like. *(Sigrun lays the blanket out and takes a big loaf of bread from her pack and lays it on the blanket.)*

ANALIESE: What are you doing?

SIGRUN: My pack is too heavy. I have a long way to go. *(She pushes it towards Analiese with her foot.)*
(Analiese takes it.)

ANALIESE: Sigrun—why did you decide to be my friend?

SIGRUN: You're stubborn. You don't complain. I like that.

ANALIESE: Would you have let Hans hurt me, if your hadn't?

SIGRUN: *(Snorts.)* No. Never. I could have sold you to the Turks as a slave. They pay in gold.

ANALIESE: Our paths may cross some time again. *(Analiese exits.)*

SIGRUN: *(She picks up Han's poem. Looks off in direction he left. Crumples paper.)* If you live. *(She waits a beat and then trails Analiese. Her knife is drawn.)*
(Analiese walks to the boat looking carefully around her. Sigrun crouches and watches. Hans enters swiftly intent on Analiese and he does not see Sigrun. Sigrun grabs him around the throat from behind.)

SIGRUN: I knew you would follow.

HANS: Get off me.

SIGRUN: Are you a dunce?

HANS: She needs protection.
(He is fighting her. Sigrun stabs him.)

SIGRUN: Yep, from you!
(He falls with a grunt and is still. Sigrun drags him away.)

SIGRUN: Viking's loved the sea. Go then. In only this are you a Viking. The ocean will be your grave.
(She starts to remove her knife. We hear children's laughter and Sigrun leaves, giving the body one last push.)

SCENE XI

Analiese and the Toucan. The boat is moving violently.

ANALIESE: The wind! What is this current? Is that the prow of a ship shattered in those rocks? We must throw ourselves out of the boat. But where? And what is this that passes? A swimmer? Hullloooooooo. It's a fish. See he has a silver fin. No look. It's a boy. He has a dagger stuck in his back. He's pitching over. Hans! Hans! Oh he's been killed.

(She tries to reach the body. The boat overturns and she tumbles out clawing her way blindly to shore. The Toucan flies to a rock on higher ground. Analiese drags herself up, coughing water.)

ANALIESE: That was Sigrun's dagger. What has she done?

(The light changes as if the sun is rising. Christian is walking down the beach playful and elated, waving a stick.)

CHRISTIAN: The mighty ocean! I will ride your back to Greenland, to Iceland. I shall see the top of the world. The China seas, Gibraltar and darkest Africa. *(He writes in the sand with a stick.)* This I swear May 5th 1898. Christian Pyndt. *(He bows.)*

(The Toucan flaps its wings.)

CHRISTIAN: (To the Toucan.) And you shall be my witness. Strange bird.

(He tries to get close. The Toucan sidles away.)

CHRISTIAN: Come here. Let me look at you. Are you puffin? Not like any puffin I've ever seen. Well you're not an auk or an eagle or a stork. Come here old fellow. I won't hurt you. What I'd give for a net. You're a pelican. Look at that bill. But those colors—you're the peacock of pelicans. I congratulate you. There…there…easy now. Why don't I just grab you and take you to one of the hunters. They'd know what the devil you are.

(He pounces, but the Toucan flies away.)

CHRISTIAN: Damn.

(The Toucan perches on a rock near Analiese. As Christian approaches he catches sight of her.)

CHRISTIAN: Oh hey there! You! help me catch that bird. *(He climbs down to her.)* *(Analiese doesn't answer.)*

CHRISTIAN: Hullo…hulloooo…person. Oh! You're a girl. I'm sorry I couldn't tell from up there…

ANALIESE: *(Looks up at him.)* Christian? *(She jumps up and hugs him tightly.)* Christian—have I found you at last!?

CHRISTIAN: *(Pulls her head back so he can looks at her. Amazed.)* Analiese?

ANALIESE: *(Hugging him.)* Where have you been for such a long time?

CHRISTIAN: Analiese. Can it really be you? Here? What are you doing here? How did you find me?

ANALIESE: Hold me. Hold me tight, so I know it's you. Oh Christian you're alive. I thought I should never see you again. *(She bursts into tears.)*

CHRISTIAN: Why are your crying, Analiese? Do I always make you cry then? You must stop. I feel like crying myself. Are you all right?

ANALIESE: I will never be all right. A boy has died because of me. Let me lie down in the sun, with my head in your lap.

(She lies down with her head in his lap. He strokes her hair.)

CHRISTIAN: A boy has died? Who was the boy?

ANALIESE: You don't know him. But he was killed.

CHRISTIAN: How did it happen? Why is it your fault?

(Analiese doesn't answer.)

CHRISTIAN: You've come so far—what has happened to you?

ANALIESE: I don't have words to tell you.

CHRISTIAN: But surely you can! You've always told me all your concerns.

ANALIESE: And you have told me none.

CHRISTIAN: So now, you'll tell me none and punish me for how I left? If this goes on—then we should never speak again.

ANALIESE: *(Singing softly.)* "The water is wide, I cannot cross over..."

CHRISTIAN: Ana, you cannot have come so far just to be a mystery to me. Tell me what has happened to you? How have you come so far to find me?

ANALIESE: *(Dreamily.)* I found a boat and followed the river. I crossed a strait and followed the coast, along the coast to a river, a flood, the ocean. Hans has died because of me. Loving is not so simple as I thought. *(She covers her face with her hands.)*

CHRISTIAN: Hush. Hush. We'll know everything in good time. *(He lifts her up and carries her off.)*

SCENE XII

Nina is sitting for a portrait, Carl Lorck sketches rapidly on a large notebook.

CARL: Turn a little to the left. Yes. And lift your chin. Perfect. *(He sketches.)* Do you want tendrils around your face or something more severe?

(Nina is preoccupied, she doesn't answer.)

CARL: Miss Iversen...

NINA: What? Oh—sketch one of each. I'll want several portraits to last the tour.

CARL: You have many admirers.

NINA: That may be, but these are for patrons. Admirers must pay their own painters if they want a portrait.

CARL: Keep your chin up, so your face is towards the light.

NINA: Like this?

CARL: Yes. If you could only bring yourself to smile. Your dimples are very pleasing.

NINA: Wasn't I smiling?

CARL: No you looked rather sad. What were you thinking about?

NINA: Nothing. Whiteness—perhaps you could paint me holding some flowers.

CARL: That's a capital idea. Any particular flower that you'd like?

NINA: Yes. Roses. Make them white. Will you be much longer?

CARL: I want to take advantage of the light. So just a few more minutes.

NINA: That means an hour.

> (Christian enters rapidly. He sees Carl and gives a stiff bow.)

CHRISTIAN: Excuse me. I didn't know you were occupied.

NINA: No. Come in. Come in. How is your friend?

CHRISTIAN: I really must talk to you.

NINA: Is she resting comfortably? She must have had an impossible journey.

CHRISTIAN: She's doing well. Thank you for your concern.

NINA: Christian, do you know Carl Lorck?

> (They give a slight bow.)

CHRISTIAN: We met briefly last week. On the beach.

CARL: Yes I was painting Mr. Moritz's daughter. It was quite lively. One of his musicians, an American dwarf named Billy, played the violin while Mr. Moritz shot ducks.

CHRISTIAN: May I speak to you alone?

CARL: She really mustn't move. We're at a crucial moment here.

NINA: *(To Carl.)* Sir?

CARL: All right then. But I can't promise how it will turn out. *(He leaves angrily.)*

NINA: Artistic temperament. But if one is to have artist friends, one learns to put up with it. Poets are the worst.

CHRISTIAN: So you have a new friend?

NINA: Carl? He's young. I don't think I want any more young friends. Older men are much more grateful.

CHRISTIAN: I'm not ungrateful.

NINA: No? What are you then?

(Christian cannot answer.)

NINA: You really must learn to put a name on your emotions. It makes them manageable—for you and for other people!

CHRISTIAN: Nina, I must take Analiese home.

NINA: Is it duty or desire?

CHRISTIAN: I hardly know. Perhaps there's no difference.

NINA: "The silence before sunrise and tears in my eyes"…is that how the song goes?

CHRISTIAN: I had hoped we'd be friends.

NINA: I see the boy who was my friend fast disappearing. What happened to the great hunter and explorer I shared so many days with? Is he skulking home with his tail between his legs?

CHRISTIAN: Nina…

NINA: I would appreciate it if you called me Miss Iversen in public. Now, I've arranged for your trip back. There will be one horse for the two of you. Maurice the baker will be accompanying you as far as Odense. He must go on to Copenhagen to see his wife, who is pregnant, by him, God willing. You can turn the horse over to Maurice when you arrive.

CHRISTIAN: Thank you. Nina…Miss Iversen…perhaps this is for the best. We are both so different.

NINA: Not so different, Christian. The monogamist and the promiscuous are quite alike when it comes to love. Both are deluded by hope.

(Analiese enters. She has cleaned up but wears the same clothes.)

NINA: Ahhh Analiese…come in.

ANALIESE: *(Curtsies.)* I came to tell you there may be no need for such sad farewells.

CHRISTIAN: It's all been arranged, Analiese. Isn't that so, Miss Iversen?

NINA: Yes. And I hope it will be more comfortable, although less daring, than your journey here.

ANALIESE: That's very generous Miss Iversen, but it may not be necessary. *(To Christian.)* I didn't come to fetch you, Christian—only to find you and make sure you were alive or not. I won't follow you around like a little girl anymore. So you don't have to leave on my account. In fact, I don't want you to. Love is too treacherous a journey for the fainthearted.

CHRISTIAN: I resent that! Just because things aren't simple, doesn't mean I'm a coward!

(Carl steps in and is about to retreat.)

NINA: Carl—have you met Miss Analiese?

CARL: *(Bows.)* Delighted Miss.

NINA: You must help me up. I fear my whole leg is cramped from sitting so long.
(Carl helps her up. She leans against him.)

NINA: Let's take a walk along the beach. The ocean is one of three things that make life worth living.
(As they exit.)

CARL: And pray—what are the other two?

NINA: *(Leaning on his arm.)* Hospitality and revenge.
(Christian and Analiese are both quiet.)

CHRISTIAN: Couldn't you have waited until we were alone to insult me like that?

ANALIESE: Were you two lovers?

CHRISTIAN: No.

ANALIESE: Do you love her still?

CHRISTIAN: We were friends.

ANALIESE: Dear friends.

CHRISTIAN: Yes. She was my dear friend!

ANALIESE: I see.

CHRISTIAN: And Hans?
(Analiese turns away.)

CHRISTIAN: I've been thinking. We should marry before we go back.

ANALIESE: Did I miss something? Was there a proposal?

CHRISTIAN: We can hardly go back to Odense together if we don't marry. In any event, we're of age now.

ANALIESE: I cannot imagine a more reluctant proposal.

CHRISTIAN: I can't help it. You appeared so suddenly. I've just gotten my first taste of adventure and I find it hard to give it up before I even see where it will take me. I have so many dreams. The thought of going home to be the good burgher husband makes me shrivel up inside. But I shall get used to it. I promise.

ANALIESE: And do you suppose I'm looking forward to staying home to fold your linen and feed the ducks? Do you think that knowing a girl who split a deer carcass and then killed a man with the same knife has left me untouched? I wish it had. Then I would never have questioned the difference between love and duty. Now that I do, I don't know what to do with myself.

CHRISTIAN: Do you mean your feelings for me are only of duty?

ANALIESE: The only home I've had all these months has been my feelings for you.

CHRISTIAN: So what are you saying?! You don't care for me any longer?

ANALIESE: I love you Christian.

CHRISTIAN: *(Relieved.)* So what could be wrong?

ANALIESE: I thought nothing of your feelings for me.

CHRISTIAN: But Ana, I love you. Always at the heart of things you've been my life.

ANALIESE: Then how could you leave?!

CHRISTIAN: I never thought of a future without you.

ANALIESE: You put me on a shelf to wait like some porcelain doll that's only played with on holidays! You haven't even kissed me.

(Christian laughs and kisses her. Once lightly. Then he kisses her again passionately.)

CHRISTIAN: Ana, Analiese—what will become of us? I have only a borrowed horse.

ANALIESE: Don't be so solemn. Not yet.

CHRISTIAN: But I have to think about us both. We must have a future.

ANALIESE: Must we decide our whole future at once? Can't we just walk and then walk some more and find some barren place where we can eat by an enormous fire and sleep on the sand?

CHRISTIAN: Like Jacob in the desert?

ANALIESE: Yes.

CHRISTIAN: What good will that do us?

ANALIESE: I don't know! Oh Christian—perhaps if we're lucky—like Jacob— we'll find a stone pillow and when we lay our heads down, perhaps we too can dream of a ladder to heaven.

END OF PLAY

DEFYING GRAVITY

———◆◀———

Jane Anderson

This play is dedicated to
that mysterious region on the other side of grief,
where loss grows wings and flies us to the light.

THE AUTHOR

Ms. Anderson grew up in Northern California and moved to New York City to be an actress. In 1975 she appeared in the New York premiere of David Mamet's *Sexual Perversity in Chicago*. She began writing when she founded The New York Writer's Block with playwrights Donald Margulies and Jeffrey Sweet. She worked as a comedienne and was among the first performers in the New York cabaret scene to fuse theater with stand-up. She moved to Los Angeles where she wrote and performed at the west-coast Ensemble Studio Theatre which produced her one-woman show *How to Raise a Gifted Child* and the first workshop production of *Defying Gravity*.

For several years Anderson made a living as a television writer which made it possible for her to return to writing for the theater full-time. Her plays to follow were *Food & Shelter, The Baby Dance, The Pink Studio, Hotel Oublietee* (recipient of the Susan Smith Blackburn Prize), *Smart Choices for the New Century*, and numerous short plays including *Lynette at 3AM* and *The Last Time We Saw Her* (both winners of the Heideman Award.) Her works have been widely produced off-Broadway and in theaters around the country, including Actors Theater of Louisville, The McCarter, Long Wharf, ACT, Pasadena Playhouse and the Williamstown Theater Festival which received a W. Alton Jones grant for an early production of *Defying Gravity*.

Ms. Anderson has also maintained a career as a respected screenwriter. Her work includes the film adaptation of *How to Make an American Quilt* and the urban fairy tale *Cop Gives Waitress $2 Million Tip*, renamed for release, *It Could Happen to You*. She received an Emmy Award and Writer's Guild Award for *The Positively True Adventures of the Alleged Texas Cheerleader-Murdering Mom*. In 1997 Anderson directed her first film, her screen adaptation of *The Baby Dance*.

She resides in Los Angeles with her partner Tess Ayers and their son Raphael.

ORIGINAL PRODUCTION

Defying Gravity was originally produced at American Place Theater on November 7th, 1997. It was directed by Michael Wilson with the following cast:

TEACHER	Candy Buckley
ELIZABETH	Alicia Goranson
BETTY	Lois Smith
DONNA	Sandra Daley
ED	Frank Raiter
C.B.	Phillip Seymour Hoffman
MONET	Jonathan Hadary

CHARACTERS

ELIZABETH: a five-year-old, played by an adult
TEACHER: her mother
MONET: the painter
C.B.: a mechanic on the NASA ground crew
DONNA: a bartender in a Cocoa Beach hang-out, African-American
BETTY & ED: a retired couple in their 60s

NOTE: a / in the dialogue means that the next speech overlaps here.

SCENE I

Lights up on Monet walking across the stage, carrying a portable easel and his paint box. In back of him we see projections of his painting of the Cathedral of Rouen.

MONET: During an exhibition of my work, I watched a woman scrutinize one of my paintings. She had her face so close to the canvas, I was afraid that she would come away with paint fixed to the end of her nose. I heard her say to her companion, I'm sorry, but there are too many colors here. I have no idea what I'm looking at. I said to her, if you step back, Madame, perhaps you'll have a better view. She did as I suggested. Oh, is it a building? Yes, It's the Cathedral of Rouen. I live in Rouen, she said, but this isn't what it looks like. This is the cathedral at dawn, I said, perhaps you were still in bed. She went to the next painting. And what is this? That is the cathedral at ten in the morning. I don't see it, she said. She went to the next. And what about this? That is the cathedral at noon. No, I still don't see it. I was about to tell the woman that she had about as much perception as a slug, when she stopped in front of a painting of the cathedral at dusk. She stared at it for a moment then said, yes, I recognize it now. You must be a very late sleeper, I said. And she looked at me with a terrible sadness in her eyes, No, Monsieur, this is the time of day when I go to light a candle for my husband. I lived long enough to see the invention of the airplane, but I never went up in one. At that time only the very brave and the very stupid were willing to fly. I once made arrangements to go up in a hot air balloon, but the fog kept us in, which was just as well because the pilot was drunk. I never saw the earth from anything higher than the bell tower of the Cathedral of Rouen. It was a wonderful view. I would have loved to have taken my paints up there, but the priest in charge was a narrow-minded wretch who believed that painters had no right to alter the perfection of God's world. What an idiot. But I always dreamed of seeing the earth from high above. Not just a bird's eye view, but God's view. And when I died, that was the last thing I had on my mind.

SCENE II

Lights up on Elizabeth as an adult.

ELIZABETH: The last time I saw my mother was in a visiting room next to the launch pad at Cape Canaveral. I remember we got there very early in the morning. They had donuts and hot chocolate waiting for us. Reporters kept coming in and my father bummed cigarettes from them. I asked my father if we were waiting for my mother to come back from space. He said that she hadn't even left yet. Then my grandmother gave me a coloring book and a new box of crayons to keep me busy. I broke the point on the blue crayon and I started to cry. *(Elizabeth gets down on the floor and starts to color with crayons.)*

TEACHER: All right, Honey, time for bed.

ELIZABETH: I'm not tired.

TEACHER: Would you put your crayons away, please?

ELIZABETH: See what I did? *(Elizabeth shows the Teacher a piece of paper filled with crayon scribbles.)*

TEACHER: I see, that's very pretty.

ELIZABETH: You know what it is?

TEACHER: No.

ELIZABETH: It's an impressed painting.

TEACHER: A what?

ELIZABETH: You know.

TEACHER: Honey, I don't.

ELIZABETH: From the book. The painting in the book.

TEACHER: Oh, you mean Impressionist?

ELIZABETH: Yeah.

TEACHER: Honey, that's wonderful.

ELIZABETH: Guess what it is.

TEACHER: Is it a flower garden?

ELIZABETH: No.

TEACHER: Water lilies?

ELIZABETH: No.

TEACHER: Clouds?

ELIZABETH: No.

TEACHER: A sunset?

ELIZABETH: Noooo. It's spaghetti!

TEACHER: Ohhh.

ELIZABETH: See?

TEACHER: I see. Come on, kiddo, it's time for bed.

ELIZABETH: I haven't touched the ceiling yet.

TEACHER: All right, are you ready? *(The Teacher lifts Elizabeth up.)* Did you touch anything?

ELIZABETH: No, I wasn't high enough.

(They do it again.)

TEACHER: Anything this time?

ELIZABETH: Uh-uh. I have to do it again.

TEACHER: Come on, you have to reach!

(Elizabeth stretches her hand up and touches something.)

ELIZABETH: Oh Mommy!

TEACHER: What did you touch?

ELIZABETH: The rings of Saturn.

TEACHER: What did they feel like?

ELIZABETH: Donuts!

TEACHER: You silly. Come on, let's brush your teeth.

ELIZABETH: Nooo.

TEACHER: Now.

SCENE III

Lights up on Betty and Ed in their Winnebago. It's night and Betty is driving. Ed is holding a map and dozing. The radio is on.

MALE RADIO ANNOUNCER: The Discovery touched down today after a successful thirteen day mission. The six crew members had a special guest on board. Ariadne the Spider, who successfully spun a web in zero-gravity. Way to go, Ariadne. In January of next year they plan to send a teacher into space. Wished they did the same with mine back in second grade. All *riiight.* You're listening to K-FARM 101, easy listening for the Dakotas.

BETTY: Honey, let's do that. Let's drive down to Florida and see a launch. I think we should.

ED: *(Vaguely.)* Florida, uh-huh.

BETTY: Are you listening?

ED: I'm listening.

BETTY: You were asleep.

ED: I'm awake.

BETTY: Are you looking for a camp ground?

ED: Yuh, uh-huh.

BETTY: You have to look for us.

ED: I am.

BETTY: I told you the other place would be full.

ED: It wouldn't have been if we had gotten there earlier.

BETTY: If we had made a reservation like I said we should.

ED: You're the one who wanted to see the Black Hills.

BETTY: What does that have to do / with anything?

ED: We don't have to go to every damn thing we see / on the map.

BETTY: We still could have called ahead. I don't know what's wrong with calling ahead.

ED: Then you should have done it.

BETTY: You wouldn't let me. Every time we passed a phone I'd want to stop
and you kept saying that we didn't have to. You wouldn't listen to me
and now look where we are.

ED: You're right, Betty, you're absolutely right.

BETTY: You know this is also very dangerous. I could fall asleep at the wheel.

ED: You aren't going to fall asleep. You're too mad at me to fall asleep.

BETTY: I'm not mad. You're the one who's mad.

ED: I'm not mad.

BETTY: The whole point of us traveling is to see things. If you don't want to
stop and look then I don't know why we're doing this, I really don't.

ED: I never said I didn't want to stop.

BETTY: You resented that we stopped for the Black Hills.

ED: Betty, the Black Hills were an extra sixty miles. I was tired of driving.

BETTY: I thought the whole point of what we're doing is to see wonderful
things. If we can't stop and see wonderful things then there's no point to
what we're doing.

ED: I'm tired, Betty, I'm just tired, that's all.

(A beat.)

BETTY: Do you think we have a good marriage?

ED: Sure, we do.

BETTY: I'm lonely, Ed. I wish you would touch me more.

(Ed his arm around Betty, briefly, pats her shoulder.)

ED: You want me to drive?

(Betty shakes her head.)

SCENE IV

The Teacher is standing in front of her class. Behind her is a projection of a cathedral.

TEACHER: It took an average of one hundred years to build a cathedral like this. Which means that the masons who laid the first stones could work an entire lifetime on the cathedral and never see it finished. Jason? *(A beat.)* Well, actually, yes, that's true, many of the workmen were killed on the job, especially in the later years of the construction when they were working at a tremendous height. *(A beat.)* Jason has brought up an interesting point, which is that some of the workmen who died were then buried in the walls of the cathedral. It was considered an honor. But no, they were not buried alive. As I was saying, it took a long time to build a cathedral and it was a very costly project. The church, which was very wealthy at the time, thought it was better to fund a cathedral than to give relief to people who were suffering from famine. Does anyone have any thoughts about that?
(No one responds.)
TEACHER: Well, think about it. Heather, would you change the slide?
(The projection changes to a picture of Monet's painting of the Cathedral of Rouen.)
TEACHER: No, Honey, that's backwards.
(The projection changes forward to a picture of a flying buttress.)
TEACHER: Stop. Thank you. All the towns were competing with each other to see who could build the tallest cathedral. And for a long time you could only build to a certain height before the pull of gravity would cause the whole thing to collapse. But then in the thirteenth century they invented the flying buttress— *(To a student.)* —butt, very funny. It broadened the base of the cathedral so the walls could rise hundreds of feet into the air. People always believed that if you defied gravity you were that much closer to God. Heather?
(The projection changes to the vast arched interior of a cathedral.)
TEACHER: Do you see? Do you see the effect it had? All the weight and stress is relieved on the outside of the building so that the inside can look like this! Do you see? Do you see how light it is? It's as if the whole interior is held up by nothing but air. And if you follow the lines of the pillars up, straight up, you are led to what many people thought was heaven. Before the airplane, this was the closest that we ever came to the experience of flight. Do you think it was worth it? *(A beat.)* Anyone?

SCENE V

Lights up on a bar in Florida. It's around ten at night. A lady bartender, Donna, is pouring a beer for C.B., who's wearing a NASA cap and a two-day growth of beard. Ed and Betty are at another table near Monet, who's sitting at his own table with a bottle of wine and a sketch book.

C.B.: *(To Donna.)* I was adjusting a bunch of nitrogen deregulators then one of the engineers shows up, tells me they changed the specifications, hands me a chart, took me an hour just to read the damn thing. Turns out they want everything back to what it was three weeks ago. These guys don't know what the fuck they're doing.

DONNA: Long day, huh?

C.B.: Oh yeah. Then I had to hassle with security so I could stay late and fix the door of my van.

DONNA: What was wrong with it?

C.B.: Hinge is broke. Every time I hit a bump the damn thing falls off. Almost wasted a jogger the other day.

DONNA: Dart board fell down again.

C.B.: Yeah, I'll take a look at it.

DONNA: What time you have to be up tomorrow?

C.B.: Three. A.M.

DONNA: What're you doin' here? You should be in bed.

C.B.: I was looking for someone to tuck me in.

DONNA: Not tonight, Sugar.

C.B.: I'm gonna work a whole lot better if I do something to clear my head.

DONNA: Try sleep.

C.B.: I'm too wound up to go to sleep.

DONNA: Uh-huh.

C.B.: Doesn't do me any good to try to sleep three hours then get up again. I might as well be doing something constructive with my time.

DONNA: Then do your laundry.

C.B.: You're breakin' my heart.

DONNA: Mine too, Baby. *(To Ed and Betty.)* Can I get you folks anything else?

ED: No, we're fine.

BETTY: We were wondering, are there any astronauts here tonight?

ED: Betty, I don't think so.

BETTY: *(Ignoring Ed.)* We were told that a lot of them like to come here.

DONNA: Well, most of them are in bed right now. They have kind of a big day tomorrow.

BETTY: Oh. Of course. *(To C.B.)* Do you work for NASA?

C.B.: Yuh.

BETTY: *(To Ed.)* Honey, he works for NASA.

ED: I could tell by the cap.

BETTY: *(To C.B.)* We're here to see the launch.

C.B.: Uh-huh.

BETTY: It's our / first time.

ED: Are you a technician?

BETTY: *(Overriding Ed.)* We've never seen a launch before. Where do you think the best place would be to see it?

C.B.: Anywhere out by the highway.

ED: *(To Betty.)* We have a good spot.

BETTY: Maybe he has one that's better.

ED: *(To C.B.)* We're out by Cocoa Beach.

C.B.: Yeh, that's a good place.

BETTY: *(To Donna.)* Are you going to see the launch?

DONNA: No Ma'am, they're too early for me. I watch the replays on TV.

ED: *(To C.B.)* Think there will be a lift-off tomorrow?

C.B.: Well, it's looking pretty good. The skies are supposed to clear up.

ED: I hear you've been having / a lot of delays.

BETTY: The weather has been terrible around here hasn't it?

C.B.: Pardon me?

BETTY: The weather.

C.B.: Yeah, it's been bad.

BETTY: I hear there've been some delays.

ED: Betty, I said that already. *(To C.B.)* So what's your position with NASA?

C.B.: Ground crew.

ED: Ah.

BETTY: *(To Donna.)* Do you know any of the astronauts?

DONNA: Yes Ma'am. *(Pointing to the wall.)* They signed that picture for me.

BETTY: *(To Ed.)* Honey, look, that's their picture.

ED: I see it.

BETTY: *(To Donna.)* What does it say?

DONNA: To Donna.

BETTY: To Donna.

ED: Uh-huh.

BETTY: Do you know the teacher? Is she nice?

DONNA: Oh yeah, she's a real good lady.

ED: *(To C.B.)* So what do you do on the ground crew?

C.B.: Right now, too much.

BETTY: It must be exciting, though, to send people up to space.

C.B.: Oh yeah.

ED: Anything interesting going up? In payload?

C.B.: Well, we've got some gizmo that's gonna measure the comet. But we've / got something going up next month...

BETTY: We're going back to Arizona to see the comet.

C.B.: Oh, uh-huh. Is that where you're from?

BETTY: No, we're from / Oregon.

ED: Oregon.

C.B.: Uh-huh.

BETTY: Ed took an early retirement and we sold our house and bought a Winnebago.

ED: I worked in engineering...

BETTY: We're traveling now. Ed loves to take pictures.

ED: I have an interest in photography...

BETTY: We started down the coast of California and we saw the Redwoods and the Gold Country and the Wine Country and then we went to San Francisco and saw the Golden Gate Bridge...

ED: A nice piece of construction...

BETTY: It's just beautiful.

ED: Got some nice shots of it in the fog...

BETTY: And then we went to Carmel in time for the butterflies...

ED: Monarch. They migrate once a year...

BETTY: And then in Big Sur we saw the whales. And then we saw Hearst Castle which was unbelievable...

ED: A lot of money went into that project.

BETTY: And then we went to Los Angeles and took the studio tours which were a lot of fun.

ED: They had a demonstration of special effects...

BETTY: And then we went over to New Mexico. I wanted to see the pueblos and Ed wanted to visit the atomic bomb site. And then we went up to Arizona to see the Grand Canyon / which was just magnificent...
(Over this, Ed wanders over to Monet and watches him sketch.)

ED: *(To Monet, re: Betty.)* That's a very good likeness. You got her expression. *(He makes a yammering motion with his hand.)*

BETTY: Then we went to Montana and went over to Yellowstone and saw Big Faithful.

ED: *Old* Faithful.

BETTY: Whatever.

C.B.: So how long you been traveling?

BETTY: Oh eight or / nine months.

ED: Eight and a half months. A long time.

BETTY: We're trying to see everything. Ed has been taking hundreds of pictures.

ED: I have about a hundred rolls so far.

BETTY: I don't know who's going to look at them.

(Ed looks to Monet for support.)

BETTY: But anyway...we've been having quite a time.

ED: *(To C.B.)* The Winnebago's been holding up very well. It's a good piece of machinery.

C.B.: Uh-huh, I hear that.

BETTY: *(To Donna.)* I'd love to go into space, wouldn't you?

DONNA: No way, I'm afraid of heights.

BETTY: So is Ed.

ED: No I'm not.

BETTY: I read that someone's already setting up tours to go into space. Is that true?

ED: It's a scam.

BETTY: No it isn't. They're doing it through Abacrombie and Fitch, I think.

DONNA: Really.

ED: *(To C.B.)* Hear they're sending a telescope up.

C.B.: Oh yeah, it's one powerful puppy. It's gonna see fifty times deeper into space than anything we've had before. *(Holding up his beer bottle.)* It can read the label on this Bud from three thousand miles away.

BETTY: Isn't that / something?

ED: When's it going up?

C.B.: Right after this launch. See, us trying to look at the stars from earth is like a bug trying to look at this room from the bottom of a can of Coke. But with that thing up in orbit, we're gonna see things we don't even know are out there...stars and galaxies and nebulae. And we're gonna see other planets, man. And we're not talking about planets from our solar system, we're talking about the planets around Alpha Centauri and the North Star. Some of them planets might look a little bit like Earth. Some of them might even have life.

BETTY: Oh my, can you imagine?

C.B.: We're gonna be seeing deep, I'm talking *deep* space. We're gonna see the light from stars that are twelve billion years old. We're gonna be seeing the creation of the universe.

(C.B. looks to see if Donna has been listening to him. She has.)

ED: This is one fine time to be alive.

C.B.: That's a fuckin' understatement. *(To Betty.)* 'Scuse me.

BETTY: That's all right.

ED: Well, time to turn in. *(To Donna.)* Miss, the check?

C.B.: *(To Donna.)* Guess I better get some sleep.

DONNA: Yeah, I guess you better.

BETTY: *(To C.B.)* We think what you people are doing is just wonderful. We'll be rooting for you.

C.B.: Thank you, Ma'am. Goodnight.

DONNA: *(To C.B.)* Hey. I'll see you later.

(C.B. smiles and leaves.)

BETTY: *(To Monet.)* Are you a writer?

MONET: No. I paint.

ED: *(To Betty.)* Come on, old gal. Time to hit the hay.

BETTY: Honey, he paints.

ED: I know. *(To Monet.)* G'night.

SCENE VI

Lights up on Elizabeth. She is holding a toy space shuttle.

ELIZABETH: That Christmas, I had asked my mother for a Cabbage Patch Doll. But she didn't have time to get me one. All the presents she got us that year were from the NASA gift shop.

(The Teacher joins Elizabeth.)

ELIZABETH: She gave me a plastic space shuttle and a package of astronaut ice cream.

TEACHER: *(To Elizabeth.)* See? It's freeze-dried!

ELIZABETH: My mother was going to read me How the Grinch Stole Christmas but she kept getting phone calls.

TEACHER: *(Into phone.)* Hello! How are you! I'm great! How are you?!

ELIZABETH: While she talked on the phone, I played with the shuttle.

(Elizabeth bangs the shuttle on the floor.)

TEACHER: *(Into phone.)* No, I don't have to go back till next week. I'm having the time of my life…hold on. *(To Elizabeth.)* Honey, what are you doing?

ELIZABETH: *(To Teacher.)* I'm trying something. *(To audience.)* I was trying to break the wing.

TEACHER: *(Back to phone.)* It's a real madhouse here. We have the family tomorrow. I thought I'd cook a roast.

ELIZABETH: Too many people were coming to the house.

TEACHER: No, thank you, we have tons of food. I keep telling everyone, if I gain anymore weight they'll have to add extra fuel just to get me off the ground.

ELIZABETH: She kept saying the same thing over and over again.

TEACHER: Well, as I've been telling everyone, I'm more nervous about getting in the car and driving on the freeway. It's a chance in a lifetime. I wouldn't miss it for the world.

(Elizabeth starts banging again.)

TEACHER: Excuse me. *(To Elizabeth.)* Elizabeth, would you please stop?

(Elizabeth throws the shuttle across the room.)

TEACHER: *(Into phone.)* Can I call you back? *(The Teacher hangs up and turns to Elizabeth.)* Pick that up.

(Elizabeth shuffles over to the shuttle and picks it up.)

TEACHER: What's gotten into you?

ELIZABETH: Nothing. *(To audience.)* She was talking on the phone too much.

TEACHER: Honey, are you bored?

ELIZABETH: I hated the shuttle.

TEACHER: Do you want Daddy to take you out with the sled?

ELIZABETH: I hated space.

TEACHER: Are you hungry?

ELIZABETH: I think at that moment, I hated her.

TEACHER: Honey, come here. Do you need a hug?

(Elizabeth goes to the Teacher, lets herself be held.)

TEACHER: Does that feel better?

(Elizabeth starts banging the shuttle against the side of her leg.)

TEACHER: Do you want to tell me what's wrong?

ELIZABETH: *(Weepy.)* I can't find my coloring book.

TEACHER: Is it in your room?

ELIZABETH: *(Still banging the shuttle.)* No.

TEACHER: *(Stopping Elizabeth's hand.)* Honey, don't. Did you look under the tree?

ELIZABETH: No, it's not there. Somebody took it.

TEACHER: Maybe your brother has seen it. Did you ask him?

ELIZABETH: I don't *want* to ask him.

(The phone rings. Elizabeth starts banging the shuttle again. The Teacher stops her hand.)

TEACHER: Elizabeth, don't do that, please.

(Elizabeth throws the shuttle at her mother.)

TEACHER: All right, that's enough. Go to your room.

ELIZABETH: *(To audience.)* I went to my room and later I came out and apologized. My mother forgave me. She blamed my behavior on Christmas.

TEACHER: *(Into phone.)* It's Christmas. You know how they get all wound up.

ELIZABETH: She took me to bed and was going to read to me about the Grinch but she got another phone call.

(Phone rings.)

TEACHER: Hello! How are you! I'm great! How are you!

ELIZABETH: My father tried to finish the story for me.

TEACHER: I'm having the time of my life...I go back next week.

ELIZABETH: I got mad and tore a page in the book. He turned the light out and told me to go to sleep.

TEACHER: I'm trying not to gain any more weight. They'll have to add extra fuel just to get me off the ground...well, as I've been telling everyone...

TEACHER AND ELIZABETH: I'm more nervous about getting in the car and driving on the freeway.

ELIZABETH: It's a chance in a life time.

TEACHER: It's a chance in a life time.

TEACHER AND ELIZABETH: I wouldn't miss it for the world.

SCENE VII

Projection: the stained glass Rose Window of Chartres Cathedral. Lights up on Teacher.

TEACHER: Even if you were very poor, you were free to walk into the cathedral and look up at something as magnificent as this. People came from hundreds of miles around on something called a pilgrimage. Can anyone tell me what it must have been like to be a pilgrim and to walk into a cathedral like Chartres? *(A beat.)* Can anyone tell me what must have gone through your mind if you had never been outside your own village and you lived in a stone hut without any windows and you couldn't read or write and you spent your days pulling a plow through the mud and you slept in the same room with your pigs and you walked two hundred miles over primitive, rocky roads in a pair of sandals that started giving you blisters after the first day and you ran out of food and a band of robbers stole your last coin and no one would even offer you a ride, and finally, *finally* you arrived at the cathedral and you saw this? *(She motions to the projection.)* Anyone? *(A beat.)* Jason? Yes, many people were burned at the stake. *(A beat.)* Yes, alive. Can we talk about that later? Heather? *(The projection changes to a picture of a reliquary.)*

TEACHER: Most cathedrals were built around a patron saint. And some of these cathedrals contained something called a relic which was held in this, a reliquary. Can someone tell me what a relic is? *(A beat.)* Patricia? *(A beat.)* That's right, a relic is a piece of the body of someone believed to be a saint. It could be a piece of bone, or some hair or even a fingernail. Yes, it is gross, but back then people believed that these remnants were—well, blessed. That if you touched them, you would be close to God. Patricia? *(A beat.)* Well, my feeling is that most of the saints were ordinary people who happened to have been put in extraordinary situations. I think it's what people said about them later on that turned them into saints. But then again, they might have been, as you said, of God. Jason? *(A beat.)* Yes, many of the saints suffered terrible deaths. Unfortunately that is one of the things that qualified a person to be a saint. In any case—can anyone think of a modern example of a relic? Anything that held some kind of magic for you? *(A beat.)* No one? Well, remember when we took that trip down to the Air and Space Museum and we stood in line to touch the moon rock? Do you remember how exciting it was to touch something that had come from the surface of the moon? Mathew? *(A beat.)* Well, I know we've been to the moon many times and brought back many rocks. But it's still a miracle that we did it at all, don't you think? *(Long beat.)* No? Oh, well then how many of you are going to fly to the moon for your summer vacation? Anyone? No? All right, then how many of you know someone who's been to the moon—your grandparents, a neighbor, a friend? No? And why do you think that is? *(A beat.)* Because it's very, very hard to get there. Thank you. All right then, one last question. If it *was* possible, if you were told that there was one free seat left on a rocket going to the moon, if you were told that you could have it, how many of you would grab the chance and go?

(The Teacher waits. We see shadows of hands appear in front of the projection as one-by-one, the children raise their hands.)

SCENE VIII

The bar. Donna and the Teacher are standing on either side of a bar stool.

TEACHER: Go ahead.

DONNA: Go ahead what.

TEACHER: Climb up.

DONNA: Uh-uh, no way.

TEACHER: What could happen?

DONNA: This thing could tip over, I could break my head.

TEACHER: You won't fall, I'll hold on to you.

DONNA: Uh-uh, can't do it.

TEACHER: Chicken.

DONNA: Hey, this is how I am. I'm an earth sign. I don't have any problem with my phobia. If I have to reach something high, I don't need a ladder, I get my boyfriend to do it.

TEACHER: What if he's not around?

DONNA: I get another boyfriend. Look, I get along just fine. My sister, she sent me a plane ticket to visit her in Pittsburgh. I said no thank you, I can drive. It only took me a day to get there. I was relaxed. I was alive. I don't need planes. Forget planes. Planes crash.

TEACHER: Oh come on, and cars don't? That is / so lame—

DONNA: I just read in the paper the other day about some jet / taking a dive off the runway—

TEACHER: How often do you get your car serviced?

DONNA: On my salary? Honey, if it ain't broke.

TEACHER: Tell me about it. But to get back to my point—

DONNA: Here she goes.

TEACHER: —flying is much safer than driving because a jet is not allowed to leave the ground until / every moving part is checked.

DONNA: Oh come on, do you think the ground crew at an airport is really doing their job?.

TEACHER: Absolutely.

DONNA: Those guys are looking at jets all day, they get bored with the routine, / their minds are wandering all over the place, they're gonna get sloppy.

TEACHER: Oh, you're such a cynic. I'm not listening to you.

DONNA: *(Over her.)* Even the ground crew here, they're the creme de la creme, but they screw up all the time—oh shit, Honey, that's not what I was trying to say. I was just—that was just me going along with the argument. I don't even know where that came from. Listen, these boys have their hearts and souls wrapped up in those rockets. I swear to the Lord, they'd rather cut their own throats than let anything happen to you.

(The Teacher just nods.)

DONNA: You want a drink?

(The Teacher shakes her head.)

DONNA: You want to put me up on this stool? I scare the crap out of you, you get to scare the crap out of me, an even exchange? So what do I do?

TEACHER: Take my hand.

DONNA: All right.

(The Teacher helps Donna up on the stool.)

DONNA: I'm too big for this.

TEACHER: No you aren't.

DONNA: I'm gonna fall.

TEACHER: I have you.

(Donna is now standing on the stool but is still bent over in a panic.)

TEACHER: Straighten up.

DONNA: Don't let go.

TEACHER: I won't. Keep your eyes open, keep looking up.

(Donna slowly straightens up.)

TEACHER: That's a girl. All right, I'm going to let go of your hand.

(The Teacher does so. Donna is standing by herself on the stool.)

DONNA: OK I did it, thank you, let me down now.

TEACHER: Not yet.

DONNA: I don't like where this is going.

TEACHER: Reach your hand up, try to touch the ceiling.

DONNA: Damn, why am I listening to you?

TEACHER: Because I'm the Teacher. Come on. Reach.

(Donna reaches her hands up.)

TEACHER: How are you doing?

DONNA: I'm doing OK.

TEACHER: Just stay up there for a minute and take in the view.

DONNA: All right.

TEACHER: What do you see?

DONNA: Oh man, there's a bunch of dead bugs on top of the TV. What'd you send me up here for? Get me down, I don't need to look at that. *(Donna gets down.)* I'm gonna send you up there next time, send you up with a broom…hey, are you all right. Oh man, is it that thing that I said? Come on sit down. What do you take, gingerale?

TEACHER: I wet my pants in training today.

DONNA: Oh don't worry about that, happens to the regulars all the time. Which ride did they put you on?

TEACHER: The escape basket.

DONNA: The one with the twenty story drop?

TEACHER: Straight down, eighty miles per hour.

DONNA: *Oh* yeah, I know about that one.

TEACHER: They told me to keep my eyes open.

DONNA: What for, the scenery?

TEACHER: I kept my eyes on my knees.

DONNA: That's the thing to do.

TEACHER: But I still lost control of myself. I was so freaked out, I didn't know my seat was wet until they pulled me out of the cage.

DONNA: There's no shame in it, Honey. Astronauts are always messing in their pants. The men who went to the moon? The whole time they were up there they were shuffling around in dirty diapers. When they came back down and they opened up the capsule? Whoo, step back!

TEACHER: It's all still very primitive, isn't it?

DONNA: Naw, it's much better now. The moon landing, they didn't know what they were doing. They got up there with duck tape and prayers. These days they've sent enough of them up, they pretty much have it down.

TEACHER: Should I be praying?

DONNA: You're asking me? Please, I pray every time I get in an elevator.

TEACHER: Do the astronauts pray?

DONNA: I always pray for them. I've never lost one yet.

TEACHER: I prayed to be chosen to go up.

DONNA: Well, there you go.

SCENE IX

Lights up on Elizabeth.

ELIZABETH: I had lost my mother once before. It was at the supermarket.
(The Teacher enters, pushing a grocery cart.)

ELIZABETH: It was late in the day and it was very crowded. I remember begging my mother to give me a quarter so I could get a Superball from the gum machine. She wanted me to stay with her and help her pick out some cereal. So I went with her to the cereal section and pointed to the Lucky Charms. But she decided we should get...

TEACHER: Nutri Grain.

ELIZABETH: She said I would like it because it had raisins.

TEACHER: Honey, you'll like it. It has raisins.

ELIZABETH: She also got a box of granola bars.

TEACHER: You can have one in the car.

ELIZABETH: I followed her to the meat department. The butcher was busy and we had to wait. I asked again for the quarter so I could buy a Superball from the gum machine. *(To Teacher.)* Mommy, please?

TEACHER: Honey, why do you want a Superball?

ELIZABETH: Because I *need* it. Please?

TEACHER: It's part of your allowance.

ELIZABETH: I don't care. *(To audience.)* She dug in the pocket of her dress and pulled out a quarter. Her right hand had blue Magic Marker on the middle finger. She kept good care of her nails, but her fingers were always marked up with pen.

(The Teacher hands her a quarter.)

ELIZABETH: The quarter was warm. I left her to go the gum machine. The machine with the Superballs was broken so I put my quarter in a machine that had creepy-crawlys. I got a green scorpion and I hated it. I went back to the meat department but my mother was gone. I went up and down the aisles, looking for her plaid dress. Mom? Mom? I listened for my mother to call back but all I could hear was the supermarket music playing, Rain drops on roses, and whiskers on kittens...Mommy? Mommy?

(Betty comes on with a cart.)

ELIZABETH: I saw a woman in a plaid dress bending down by the soups. *(To Betty.)* Mommy?

BETTY: What do you want, little girl?

ELIZABETH: I ran to the check-out counters and went from register to register looking for my mom. I saw a box of Nutri Grain moving on a conveyor belt.

(Ed is standing in line.)

ELIZABETH: But the Nutri Grain was followed by a bag of prunes and an old man was pulling out his wallet. I ran to the parking lot to see if my mother was in the car. But a man came through with a bunch of carts.

(C.B. comes barreling towards her with a stack of carts.)

C.B.: Coming through! Coming through!

ELIZABETH: And he didn't see me and he almost ran me over and I started to cry. I ran back to the check-out counters and I saw a little girl standing there with her mother. And her mother handed her a granola bar. And I knew I would never have a granola bar again because I went to the gum ball machine and got a green scorpion which I hated and I didn't even have the quarter my mother gave me which was still warm from the pocket of her dress, the quarter that my mother's hand had touched with the Magic Marker on the middle finger, I lost it *(Crying hysterically.)* MOMMEEEEEE! MOMMEEEEE! I WANT MY MOMMEEEE! GIVE ME BACK MY MOMMY!!!!

(The Teacher enters with her cart.)

TEACHER: Elizabeth?

ELIZABETH: Mommy, I couldn't find you! I looked everywhere! You were gone! I thought you went home! I thought you left me!

TEACHER: Silly, why would I leave without you? Why would I do that?

(Elizabeth is still sobbing. The Teacher holds her.)

TEACHER: It's all right, sweet girl, I'm right here, it's all right. We'll be home in a little while.

ELIZABETH: I stayed very close to the cart.

(Elizabeth puts her hand on the handle next to the Teacher's hand. They start pushing the cart together across the stage.)

ELIZABETH: And when we got in the car, she gave me a granola bar.

SCENE X

Lights up on Betty and Ed on a beach. Betty is sitting in a plastic lawn chair. Ed is setting up his camera on a tripod. Apart from them is Monet, painting at his easel. Betty keeps looking over at him, desperately wanting to see what he's painting.

BETTY: Are you here for the launch?

MONET: Yes.

BETTY: Are you from around here?

MONET: No, I am from France.

BETTY: France. Oh, I've always wanted to go to France. I love the Impressionists, don't you?

MONET: You know of them?

BETTY: Oh yes. Ed and I saw the Van Gogh exhibit in New York. I bought some of his note cards.

MONET: Van Gogh?

BETTY: He did that famous painting, Starry Starry Night? He was disturbed but quite brilliant.

MONET: Yes, I know of him.

(Betty looks at what he's painting.)

BETTY: You're very good.

MONET: Thank you.

BETTY: You know, if I had tried to paint that scene I would have made it all gray and brown. But look at all those colors. Do you actually see those colors or do you make them up?

MONET: No, Madame, they are all there.

BETTY: *(To Ed.)* Honey, you should see what he's doing. He's very good.

ED: Betty, I'm sure the man would like to be left alone. *(To Monet.)* She does the same thing to me when I'm trying to take a photograph. She's always telling me where to point.

BETTY: Well, sometimes you need direction. *(To Monet.)* He takes too many pictures of horizons.

ED: What the hell else am I supposed to take. *(To Monet.)* Horizons are a good point of reference, am I right?

MONET: Oh yes. They are hard to ignore. But there comes a time when you have to let them go.

(Ed watches Monet paint for a beat.)

ED: *(Shyly.)* I used to paint. Water colors. I would of liked to have done it full time, but well, you know...

MONET: I understand.

ED: I still have the eye for it though. *(Squinting up at the sky.)* That's one heck of a blue, isn't it?

MONET: It most certainly is.

BETTY: *(To Monet.)* Wouldn't you just love to paint from outer space?

MONET: Very much.

BETTY: You know, once when Ed and I flew cross-country to visit our son and daughter-in-law in Connecticut, I spent the whole time looking out the window. It was the most beautiful view I'd ever seen. I loved the farm land—all those fields in different colored squares. It looked like a giant patch-work quilt. I kept thinking to myself, wouldn't it be wonderful if someone like Van Gogh were sitting next to me and he could look out the window and see what I'm seeing. Has that ever occurred to you?

MONET: About Van Gogh? No.

ED: Betty, have you seen my lens paper?

BETTY: Did you check the glove compartment?

ED: Yes.

BETTY: What about your camera case?

ED: That's where it was supposed to be.

BETTY: Well, Honey, I don't know.

MONET: I believe it's in your coat pocket next to your glasses.

(Ed checks his coat and pulls out the lens paper.)

ED: Well, I'll be.

(Monet begins to pack up his easel.)

BETTY: If you want to keep painting, we'll let you alone.

MONET: I am done for now.

BETTY: The launch is about to start. Don't you want to stick around?

MONET: It won't happen today. *(He takes Betty's hand and kisses it.)* It was a pleasure, Madame. I will try to do as well as your Mr. Van Gogh. *(To Ed.)* A friend of mine, Victor Hugo, once said: The horizontal is the line of reason, the vertical is the line of prayer. Don't worry about your horizons. Someday, you won't even know it, they will disappear.

SCENE XI

Lights up on Elizabeth.

ELIZABETH: The day my mother actually left, a reporter asked me what I thought of my mother going into space. I didn't want to answer so I hid my face behind my grandmother's purse. My brother laughed at me so I hit him on the arm. My grandmother gave us Lifesavers to quiet us down. I told her I wanted a cherry so she peeled the paper down until she found one for me. I put it in my pocket for later. Then my mother joined us and she let me hold her hand while she talked to the reporters. I played with her wedding ring and I was very proud that I was one of the few people who was allowed to touch her hand. She showed the reporters some of the things she was taking up to space. She had a journal and in the journal was a bookmark that I made for her. I had drawn a rocket and stars and Saturn with the rings and I ironed it between two pieces of wax paper so it would be protected from the gamma rays. Then she showed the reporters something her class had given her. I was jealous and I wanted to give her something else. So I took out the Lifesaver. It was fuzzy from the lining of my pocket. While my mother and the reporters talked, I tried to make the Lifesaver presentable. I told myself that I had to pick all the lint off the Lifesaver or my mother wouldn't come back. Finally my mother crouched down next to me. She was wearing her blue space suit. I touched the patches on her shoulders. She looked so beautiful. Suddenly I couldn't grasp that this woman was the same person who every morning sliced banana on my granola. My grandmother kept saying, say good-bye, honey, say good-bye to your mother. But all I could manage to do was to hold out the Lifesaver. My mother took it and put it in her pocket and I knew that everything would be all right.

SCENE XII

Lights up on the Teacher strapped into her shuttle chair which is angled all the way back in the take-off position so that she's flat on her back.

NASA VOICE ON SHUTTLE RADIO: ...T-minus thirty minutes and counting. Checking fuel valves.

(Monet appears, carrying his portable easel and paint box. He's holding a book mark.)

MONET: Madame? Madame, you dropped this.

TEACHER: Oh, thank you. Are we in space yet?

MONET: No, not yet.

TEACHER: What am I thinking, everything would be floating by now, wouldn't it. You aren't floating, are you?

MONET: Only in time, Madame.

TEACHER: Are you coming with us?

MONET: I plan to, yes. *(To his easel.)* Do you know where I might put this?

TEACHER: Oh gosh, I'm not sure. They don't give you a lot of storage space in here. Are those your paints?

MONET: Yes.

TEACHER: I might have room in my locker for a couple of your tubes but I don't think you'll be able to take your easel. You won't really need it up there anyway.

MONET: No, of course I won't. How silly of me.

TEACHER: *(The bookmark.)* Did you see this? My little girl made it for me.

MONET: Yes, it's quite marvelous. *(Reading.)* E-li-za-beth.

TEACHER: Oh my God, I didn't see that. She wrote her name. You don't know what a big thing this is for her. I've been trying to help her learn it but she said she couldn't because I gave her a name with too many letters in it. She gets so frustrated, she always tears up the paper. This is such a big step for her. Oh my sweet girl. I should have paid more attention when she gave it to me.

NASA VOICE ON SHUTTLE RADIO: T-minus twenty-eight minutes and counting. Fuel system is functioning.

TEACHER: Is there a phone up here? I have to call her. I have to call her or she'll think I didn't care. *(The Teacher tries to unbuckle herself.)* I can't get out of this. Can you help me?

MONET: I will try but I'm afraid that I'm not very mechanical.

TEACHER: Please hurry, I need to get out of here.

MONET: I am trying, Madame.

TEACHER: I need to see her. I need to see my little girl.

NASA VOICE ON SHUTTLE RADIO: T-minus twenty-six minutes and counting. Checking auxiliary wing flaps.

MONET: I'm so sorry, but I can not open the buckle.

NASA VOICE ON SHUTTLE RADIO: Auxiliary wing flaps are functioning. Checking main wing flaps.

TEACHER: Oh God, will she ever forgive me?

MONET: Do not despair, Madame.

NASA VOICE ON SHUTTLE RADIO: T-minus twenty-four minutes and counting. Main wing flaps are functioning. Checking right tail flaps.

(Monet has left. The book mark slips out of the Teacher's hand and falls to the ground.)

NASA VOICE ON SHUTTLE RADIO: Right tail flaps are functioning. Checking left tail flaps.

(The Teacher tries to retrieve the bookmark but she can't reach because of the restraints. Lights start to fade.)

NASA VOICE ON SHUTTLE RADIO: Left tail flaps are functioning, checking rudder...

SCENE XIII

Fade up on Betty and Ed on the beach waiting for the launch. Ed is making last-minute adjustments on his camera which is set up on a tripod. Betty is listening to a portable radio.

NASA VOICE ON RADIO: ...T minus fifteen seconds and counting... / no unexpected errors.

BETTY: Do you think it will actually go up this time?

ED: Well, I'll believe it when I see it.

NASA VOICE ON RADIO: T-minus 14...13...12...11... / 10...9...8...7...6... 5...we have main engine start...

BETTY: Where are we supposed to be looking?

ED: It should be coming up about twenty degrees to the south.

BETTY: That doesn't mean anything to me, Ed. Do I look straight ahead or to the right, or what?

ED: *(Pointing impatiently.)* Over there, just look over there.

NASA VOICE ON RADIO: *(Over this.)* ...4...3...2...1...and lift off. We have lift off of the twenty-fifth space shuttle mission. And it has cleared the tower. *(Ed looks through his camera, starts clicking. We hear the distant roar of a rocket.)*

BETTY: There it is! I see it! Oh my God! Look at it! Oh Ed, look at it go! *(Ed is madly clicking and advancing the film.)*

ASTRONAUT VOICE ON RADIO: Houston, we have roll program.

NASA VOICE ON RADIO: Roger, roll Challenger.

BETTY: Isn't it beautiful! It's just beautiful! How do they do it?! Oh my God, it's just magnificent.

NASA VOICE ON RADIO: Challenger, go with throttle up.

ASTRONAUT VOICE ON RADIO: Roger, go with throttle up. *(An explosion. Betty looks puzzled. Ed looks up from his camera.)*

BETTY: Was that supposed to be part of it?

NASA VOICE ON RADIO: One minute, fifteen seconds. Velocity twenty-nine thousand feet per second. Altitude nine nautical miles. Downrange distance seven nautical miles.

BETTY: *(Over this.)* Are they all right? *(Ed doesn't say anything, stares at the sky.)*

BETTY: Oh my God, oh Ed, my God. Oh my God. *(Ed puts his arm around Betty and leads her off. Then:)*

NASA VOICE: Flight controller here looking very carefully at the situation. Obviously a major malfunction.

SCENE XIV

Lights up on the Teacher. She is facing the kids holding a cage with a dead Guinea Pig inside.

TEACHER: All right, everybody let's quiet down. That's enough. Let's try to find out what happened here.

C.B.: I think I figured out what happened here.

TEACHER: Five of you were responsible for feeding Miss Piggy.

C.B.: Sixteen thousand of us were responsible for getting one rocket into space.

TEACHER: All right, who had Monday? Heather was supposed to be Monday.

C.B.: And all of us were divided into different departments, see? And every department was divided up into divisions and mini divisions and mini-mini divisions.

TEACHER: Heather, if you forgot to feed Miss Piggy on Monday, then you should have told the person on Tuesday so they could have given her extra food. Who had Tuesday? One at a time!

C.B.: And every division had it's own technical language, see. For instance, there's this little plastic part the size of my pinkie.

TEACHER: All right, Mathew was sick on Tuesday. And what about Wednesday? Anyone?

C.B.: The guys in tiles and O-rings call it a C-scale Oxidizer.

TEACHER: Who was Thursday? Jennifer?

C.B.: The guys in air locks call it an OMS Regulator. And over in propulsion they call it a Preburner Fuel Thrust.

TEACHER: Someone told you it was for every other week?

C.B.: Hell, I just call it a valve.

TEACHER: Who was Friday? *(A beat.)* I never said I was Friday. Did I?

C.B.: So this is the point. See, it's just like the Tower of Babel.

TEACHER: Has anyone heard of the Tower of Babel? *(To a boy.)* Jeffrey, can you tell us?

C.B.: OK, a long time ago everyone in the world was gonna get together and build this big tower, right? They were building it 'cause they were trying to reach heaven. And they started building this thing and it was goin' really well and it got higher and higher. And God got really nervous and He...

TEACHER: Or She, go on...

C.B.: ...wanted to figure out a way to stop them.

TEACHER: That's right.

C.B.: So God made all the people who were working on the tower…

TEACHER AND C.B.: …speak in different languages.

TEACHER: And the people who sawed the wood couldn't understand the people who mixed the mortar.

C.B.: And the guys in mortar couldn't understand the guys in brick. And the guys in brick couldn't understand the guys in dry wall and everyone started running around and…

TEACHER: *(and C.B.)* …shouting at each other and no one knew who was supposed to do what, and everyone started making mistakes *(Fucking up.)*

TEACHER: …and the wrong nail was put in the wrong board…

C.B.: …and the wrong board was hammered to the wrong beam.

TEACHER AND C.B.: And the whole thing came crashing down.

C.B.: The whole damn thing came down.

TEACHER: We have to speak clearly to each other. Or else, look what happens? *(She holds up the cage.)*

C.B.: That's what happened.

TEACHER: Jennifer, would you take Miss Piggy to the janitor?

C.B.: …too many damn departments. But it was still my fault.

TEACHER: No, Jason, you can not have the bones.

SCENE XV

Lights up on C.B. holding a letter.

C.B.: *(Reading.)* Dear Elizabeth, I'm writing to you on behalf of the men who worked on the ground crew of shuttle flight 51-L. We want you to know how much all of us admired your mother and we offer our sincerest condolences to you and your family. *(He puts the letter down.)* I volunteered to write this letter 'cause I feel partly responsible for what happened. I don't know what you remember, but there were a lot of false starts before your mom's ship finally got off the ground. Some of the delays had to do with the weather, but one of the delays had to do with human error. This human error delay took place on a day that would of been perfect for a lift off. The weather was clear and the sky was a beautiful bright blue. It was as if God just lifted up a giant man-hole cover and said aim here. Well, at T minus nine minutes they couldn't get the handle off of one of the hatches and they had to get this special drill. But when that arrived it didn't work 'cause someone used it and didn't bother to replace the batteries. Let me just explain the situation. See, I borrowed the drill to fix the door on my van. So after work I used the drill then I stuck a note on it saying to change the batteries. But I used a Post-it that I took off someone's door and the sticky stuff on the back was kinda used up and I guess it didn't stay on the drill. I should of just changed the batteries myself but in order to do that I would of had to fill out a form explaining why I needed the new batteries and then I'd have to run it over to another building to get it approved, then wait an hour to have it processed then go to another building to pick the batteries up, then I would of had to get a guy to supervise me while I put the batteries in and hell, I was at the end of a twenty hour shift of regulating a bunch of LOX bleed valves and my next shift was in five hours. So instead I went to a local place to wind down. It's a place where a lot of us hung out with your mom and the other astronauts. Once, I played her a game of darts. She beat the heck out of me. You would of been proud. She also won the football pool. What I'm trying to say here is that we saw your mom every day. The last thing any of us wanted to do was to send her up in a ship that was gonna fall apart. I'm sorry. I'm so sorry. I never meant to take your mommy away from you. *(Going back to the letter.)* She was a great example to us all and will live long in our memories as a pioneer of our times. We extend our best wishes for your future and hope that as your mother did, you will be able to follow your dreams. Sincerely Yours, C.B. Williams and the men of Ground Crew number 7749, Division Eighty-six, Department K699-99, Kennedy Space Center.

SCENE XVI

Lights up on Betty and Ed, beach combing. Monet is drawing in the sand with his staff.

BETTY: *(To Monet.)* Apparently this is a good beach for scraps. This man told us that he used to come down here during the Mercury program when they were testing all those rockets? He said the darn things were blowing up every other day and they'd fall in the ocean and the tide would bring them up right here. He said he'd come here and pick up the pieces and then bring them home and mount them on plaques. I thought it was a little strange, but as Ed explained it, it's like owning a little / piece of history.

ED: A little piece of history. *(Ed is examining something.)*

BETTY: Honey, what is that? Do you have something?

ED: I don't know.

BETTY: Let's see. It's kind of rubbery isn't it? Maybe it's a piece of the shuttle. Oh my God, it is. Look Ed, that's what it is.

ED: No, I think it's a piece of a rubber thong.

BETTY: Oh. Oh well. *(To Monet.)* You know what upsets me so much about what happened? It wasn't only the loss of those wonderful lives—every time I think about them I want to weep—but what makes me very sad is that I now know that Ed and I will never take a trip to space. All those things that we thought were going to happen, they're out of our lifetime now.

(Monet picks something up.)

BETTY: Did you find something? Let's see. *(Examines it.)* Huh. No it isn't anything. It's just a Lifesaver.

(She walks away. Monet puts the Lifesaver in his pocket.)

SCENE XVII

Lights up on the bar. Donna is cleaning up. C.B. is drunk.

C.B.: P.F. Flyers. Do you remember those?

DONNA: Uh-huh.

C.B.: If you put them on you could fly. Remember that?

DONNA: Oh yeah.

C.B.: I remember the TV ad. They showed a kid putting on a pair of P.F. Flyers and then he'd walk out of the shoe store and jump over a building. We believed it. Every kid who watched that ad believed it. I jumped off a roof in a pair of those shoes. Those fucking shoes. I knew a kid who got himself killed 'cause of those God damn shoes.

DONNA: C., I'm closing up soon.

C.B.: They're scrapping the telescope, did I tell you that?

DONNA: Yeah, you did. I'm gonna drive you home, OK?

C.B.: No, I'm fine.

DONNA: You're in no condition, Hon.

C.B.: I gotta get rid of my van. The fuckin' door won't stay on. I killed seven people to fix that door and the God damn thing keeps falling off, can you dig that?

DONNA: Listen, Sugar, I hate to be the one to tell you, but you're not that important. You had nothing to do with what happened. Maybe there are a few puny things down here that you can control, but there's a master plan out there that you can't read, let alone change. Maybe we weren't meant to send that telescope up. Maybe there's something out there God doesn't want us to see. Maybe He thinks we just aren't ready.

C.B.: I wouldn't of screwed up if you let me get my sleep that night.

DONNA: Excuse me?

(C.B. doesn't say anything.)

DONNA: How dare you? Don't you go putting blame on my head. You want to climb on the cross for this one go ahead, but I'm not having any part of it. You understand? I've had it with you. Go call yourself a cab.

(Donna pushes C.B. off the bar stool. He walks off. Donna turns to the audience.)

DONNA: A reporter came in here, wanted to know, what was the last thing the astronauts said to me. What did they *say* to me?, I said. Yes, he said, exactly what did each of them say to you that last night when they left the bar? *(A beat.)* Goodnight Donna, Goodnight, Night. Goodnight Donna. Night, Donna, Goodnight.—was that seven? Oh right, one more, Good night. He actually wrote all of that down. Then he wanted to know if I remembered anything else they might have said to me, it didn't have to be that particular night, any little tidbits, he said. I said, Honey, a tidbit is something you feed to a dog. He then amended himself, asked, did any of them *confide* in me. Yes they did, I said, but confide comes from confidential and it will remain that way. I could see the hair in his ears start to vibrate with excitement, ooh, this lady has tidbits! How am I gonna get them out of her? He decides to distract me, he looks over at the picture I have of my astronauts, What's that?, he says. It was such a dumb-ass question I didn't even bother to answer, just kept wiping the bar. You must have felt very close to all of them, he said. I just kept wiping. Then he leaned in towards me, real close, trying to get into some confidence with me, he says, do you think they *knew?* I just kept wiping and wiping the bar until he went away. *(A beat.)* One of my astronauts noticed that I keep a Bible behind the bar. And this individual sat with me late one night and we talked about the afterlife. This individual was experiencing a moment of fear. This individual had doubts. I told this individual what I believe to be the truth: that the one thing we know about death, is that we all got to do it. And when and where we do it is left in the hands of God. And those who do it go on to a much higher place than those who are left behind. Those who do it are released of their bonds. Those who do it will finally know the secrets of the universe. And isn't that after all why some fool would want to put themselves on top of a rocket in the first place?

SCENE XVIII

Lights up on Elizabeth.

ELIZABETH: When I watched my mother's ship take off, I saw it go straight into the sky and disappear. When my grandmother told me that my mother went to heaven, I thought that heaven was a part of outer space. I was excited because I thought she'd come back with all kinds of neat presents like a plastic harp or a pair of angel wings. I went to the mail box every day looking for a post card from her that would have clouds on it or a three-D picture of God. I waited for her to call long distance. When I didn't hear from her, I got very angry. I told my father that I hated her for being away so long. He told me that she had perished in the rocket. I told him that wasn't true, that she was alive. That she had left us and found a family that she liked better. He asked me why did I think she was still alive. And I said, because I never saw her dead. These are the reasons I gave myself for why my mother didn't come back. One: I hit my brother on the arm. Two: I wouldn't talk to the reporters. Three: I didn't say thank you to my Grandma for giving me the coloring book. Four: I wouldn't let my father hold me. And five: I didn't get all the lint off the Lifesaver. *(Elizabeth sits on the floor with her crayons and the scribbled drawing we saw earlier.)*
(Monet enters and looks down at the drawing.)
MONET: Ah. Spaghetti?

SCENE XIX

Monet and Elizabeth. Projection of one of Monet's paintings of the gardens at Giverny.

MONET: My mother was a wonderful gardener. When I was a little boy I used to help her. I got a half a centime for every snail I killed. She had every kind of flower imaginable. Hollyhocks and columbine, tulips, lilies, pansies, Sweet William, Forget-me-nots. Her favorite flowers were poppies. They were very big, very bright. Orange and red. Fantastic colors. She told me, Claude, the secret to poppies is to plant them firmly in the ground. If the roots are firmly set, then the flowers will grow tall. And never water them from above or the flowers will be weighted down by the drops which would defeat the purpose of the poppy, because the purpose of the poppy is to float above the other flowers. They are nature's balloons. Whenever I would cut them, I held tightly on to the stems for fear that they would float away. My mother died when I was ten. Her last words to me were, I love you Claude…don't forget the snails. After she died, I wouldn't have anything to do with her garden. In two weeks, the snails had chewed everything down to the stems. My mother's garden was lost. I took great pains to punish myself for my neglect. I went to confession. I wouldn't take dessert. I wore my woolen coat without a shirt. I offered to cut my father's toe nails. But the next Spring, everything started to bloom again. I killed the snails and I brought my mother's garden back to life. One day in late Spring, the sun was warming the air and the most wonderful perfume rose up from the garden. It was my mother's scent. And I felt my mother bending next to me, guiding my hand as I dug in the earth. And I felt her breath in my ear, and she whispered, Claude, always turn the soil in the spring, don't hurt the worms, feed the roses twice a year and please, don't ever water poppies from the top. *(Monet digs in his pocket and pulls out the Lifesaver. He carefully picks a piece of lint off then hands it to Elizabeth and walks off.)*

SCENE XX

Elizabeth holds the Lifesaver up. We hear tacky circus music. Elizabeth turns to the audience.

ELIZABETH: About a year after my mother died my father took us to the Mingus Family Circus. Even at that age my brother and I could tell it was a pretty raunchy operation. The men who set up the tents and shoveled the elephant poop all had tattoos and bad teeth. My brother told me they were all drug addicts. At intermission I stayed in the tent and watched them set up the trapeze for the high wire act. About a dozen of them ran around fitting metal poles into the ground and hoisting lines of rope. I saw two of them trying to keep a giant metal pole taut against the wires. It wasn't long enough so they stuck a rubber tire under it. That didn't work so they kept slipping pieces of wood between the tire and the pole, like you slip match books under a table leg to keep it from wobbling. I thought maybe I should tell someone about this but then the lights dimmed and my brother pulled me back to my seat.

(Monet steps out, wearing a top hat.)

MONET: Ladies and Gentlemen, Boys and Girls, if you will direct your attention to above the ring, the Mingus Family Circus proudly presents the Fearless First Family of Flight, the Flying Hernandez!

ELIZABETH: And then the Hernandezes came out, dressed in blue tights and sparkles and smiling and waving. They were nice looking people. I wanted to run up and grab them and shout, Don't fly! Don't fly! Something will happen, don't fly! But I just sat there and ate my brother's popcorn and watched as the Flying Hernandezes shed their capes and climbed up the ropes. As the first Hernandez stepped up on the tiny platform, thirty feet above, I waited for the wood to crack and send him hurling to the ground. And when that didn't happen, I watched as the head Hernandez grabbed the trapeze and swung out. I knew that the wires would snap and send him sailing through the top of the tent, leaving a hole in the canvas in the shape of his body. And when that didn't happen, I knew that we were only waiting for the biggest disaster of all.

MONET: Ladies and Gentlemen if I can have your attention please. The Flying Hernandez are about to perform their famous simultaneous triple somersault. We request that you please remain absolutely silent for the duration of their act.

(A drum roll.)

ELIZABETH: Everyone in the tent was still. The only thing that was moving was the head Hernandez who was swinging back and forth by his knees and flexing his hands. I wondered if he knew about the rubber tire and the wooden blocks. I wondered if he knew that they were all about to be killed.

(Drum roll continues for a beat, then TA-DA.)

ELIZABETH: But it didn't happen. The head Hernandez was now sitting on his trapeze, swinging back and forth like a kid at a playground. And I realized that something truly remarkable had just happened. That despite the bad rigging and the degenerate ground crew, the Hernandezes were still alive.

(C.B. rolls a tall ladder on to the stage. Monet starts to climb the ladder.)

ELIZABETH: And it was at that point that the Head Hernandez looked down at me and said...

MONET: Come up, come on up!

(Elizabeth hesitates, looks at C.B. who's holding on to the ladder.)

C.B.: Go on, I have you. I swear on my life.

(Elizabeth looks up at Monet who nods to her that it's all right. As she starts to climb the ladder a projection of the horse-head nebulae comes into view.)

C.B.: IT'S UP! THEY GOT IT UP! GOD DAMN! THEY GOT THE TELESCOPE UP! WE'RE GONNA SEE TO THE EDGE OF THE UNIVERSE!

SCENE XXI

Lights up on Donna and C.B. sitting on a swing. C.B. guides a giant telescope over to her.

C.B.: OK, you see in the upper left hand corner of that dark part that looks kinda like a horse?

DONNA: *(Looking.)* A horse...you mean a whole horse?

C.B.: No, just his head.

DONNA: Oh, OK, I see it...

C.B.: Now just to the right, on his nose, is that real bright part?

DONNA: Uh-huh...

C.B.: Now count three stars up from that. *(A beat.)* You have it?

DONNA: Uh-huh, I think so...

C.B.: The third star to the right...take a look at it.

DONNA: I'm looking...

C.B.: You see anything around that star?

DONNA: Not yet...

C.B.: Keep looking.

(Donna suddenly gasps.)

DONNA: Oh my God.

C.B.: Pretty amazing isn't it?

DONNA: C.B., oh my God.

C.B.: You're the first one I've shown it to.

DONNA: I can't believe it.

C.B.: I wanted you to see it.

DONNA: It's blue. And it has clouds.

C.B.: Yep, just like ours.

DONNA: I can see oceans. And land...

C.B.: Kinda pretty, isn't it?

DONNA: It's like a beautiful blue marble. It's out there. Oh my God.

C.B.: I named it after you. Donna. The planet Donna.

DONNA: Oh Baby, you got me a planet?

C.B.: Yep.

DONNA: You're too much.

C.B.: You like it?

DONNA: My God, look at it. It's full of life.

C.B.: Just like you, Precious.

DONNA: *(To the planet.)* Hello! We see you! Hello!

C.B.: HELLO DONNA!

DONNA: HELLO!

C.B.: DONNA HELLO!

C.B. AND DONNA: Hellooo! HELLOOOOOOO! HELLOOOOOOO!
(As lights fade on C.B. and Donna, the projection dissolves to a shot of the Earth from space.)

SCENE XXII

The projection changes to another shot of the Earth as seen from the surface of the moon. Projection changes to an out-of-focus shot of the moon. Lights up on Betty and Ed sitting in their lawn chairs in front of the screen. Ed has one of those automatic slide changes in his hand. He clicks it. Projection: another fuzzy shot of the moon.

BETTY: Ed, how many of these did you take?
(Click. Projection: another bad shot.)

BETTY: Honey, I thought you sorted these.
(Click. Projection: another bad shot.)

ED: *(To audience.)* I think this one was from the Sea of Tranquillity.
(Click. Projection: an out-of-focus Earth rising over the moon.)

BETTY: Honey, what happened?

ED: I was trying a different lens.

(Click. Projection: the famous picture of footprints on the moon.)

ED: That's a shot of man's first step on the moon.

BETTY: *(To audience.)* He bought that one.

(Click. Projection: a shot of Betty floating.)

BETTY: Oh, now this is me in our hotel room. It orbits the Earth every twenty minutes.

ED: Ninety minutes.

BETTY: Ninety minutes. We stayed in the zero-gravity wing of the hotel. They don't have any beds in the room. You just shut your eyes and float. Ed was always dozing off.

ED: Well, you tired me out. *(To audience.)* You get a lot of honeymooners up there.

BETTY: *(Embarrassed.)* Well, of course, that too.

ED: *(To audience.)* Would you like to know what it's like?

BETTY: Ed, stop.

ED: *(To Betty.)* They'd like to know.

BETTY: I don't think so.

ED: *(To audience.)* It was the best experience in our marriage that we ever had. .

BETTY: It was very nice.

ED: That's not what you said to me.

BETTY: Well. *(To audience.)* At first it was silly. It was very silly.

ED: *(To audience.)* It takes some practice. You can't make any sudden moves.

BETTY: It can be dangerous. I almost killed poor Ed.

ED: That's right, she almost killed me.

BETTY: I accidentally kicked his leg and he went sailing into the air lock hatch. *(To Ed.)* You remember our clothes?

ED: That was pretty wild.

BETTY: *(To audience.)* We didn't put our clothes away so they just hung there—

ED: In mid air.

BETTY: And the more we moved, the more the clothes would tumble around.

ED: Tumble around.

BETTY: And they kept tangling up in our feet. It was like being inside a giant washing machine.

ED: It's like being under water.

BETTY: That's right, under water.

ED: Betty looked like a mermaid.

BETTY: Oh, stop.

ED: Her hair was floating out from her head and her bosoms...

BETTY: Ed...

ED: ...her bosoms had a life of their own.

BETTY: You thought I was funny-looking. You should have seen what you looked like.

ED: I didn't say you were funny-looking. You were beautiful.

BETTY: So anyway....

ED: Anyway...

BETTY: It was very silly.

ED: But once we figured out what we were doing...

BETTY: Honey, they've heard enough.

ED: You see, on Earth, everything is horizontal or vertical but in space it's 3-D. Even with a bad back the variety is endless.

BETTY: Ed.

ED: What was it you said to me?

BETTY: I don't remember.

ED: Betty said, the best thing about making love in outer space is that you don't have to worry about who's on top.

BETTY: It's true. *(Betty takes Ed's hand.)* We had two windows in the room. On one side we looked out at space. On the other side we looked down at the Earth. Ed held me and we watched the sun set and then a few minutes later, we saw it rise again. And on the other side was the whole universe spread out before us with the brightest stars we'd ever seen. We were suspended next to each other, very still, feeling no weight. Like we weren't two people anymore but two spirits...

ED: Two spirits...

BETTY: Who had floated up from Earth.

SCENE XXIII

Projection: A shot of the Earth taken from the shuttle—a grand vista of clouds scattered across land and ocean. Lights up on Monet floating across the stage.

MONET: I had to master the conditions of space before I could start to paint. One can't simply throw one's brush down and pick up another as you do on Earth, as anything you put aside will float away. But thanks to a wonderful material called Velcro, I've been able to keep my tubes fastened to my smock. However I do tend to lose track of the caps and must hunt them down like butterflies when I'm done. The paint itself is thick enough so that if I'm careful it will stay adhered to the palette. But sometimes in my enthusiasm I will squeeze a tube too hard and the paint will float away from me in the form of a brightly colored snake. The view outside the window is quite intriguing. There is no horizon line to speak of. Just patterns of clouds and land and sea and a clear, fantastic light. Every ninety minutes we circle the Earth and I have the pleasure of watching sixteen sunsets a day. My only regret is that it passes by so fast. When I painted my series of the cathedral, I used to be enormously frustrated with the rapid change of light but the time I had then was luxurious compared to what I have now. So I've lined up six canvasses in a row and I work on each section of the Earth as we sail by. And when we pass into night I load up my palette with paint so I'm ready to start back on canvas number one. I have fifteen orbits in which to finish my paintings until the Earth shifts into another time of day. I plan to paint every piece of Earth in every kind of light. I'm very much looking forward to seeing the Mediterranean at sunrise and I hear that the French Alps are quite spectacular at dusk. I have been painting for four straight days now. I have no desire to eat or sleep. My body is no longer of consequence. I have only eyes and a hand and a brush and paint and the sun endlessly bouncing colors off the Earth. And I will continue to paint as long as this wonderful rocket will keep me in space.

SCENE XXIV

Lights up on the Teacher and Elizabeth standing together, high up on the ladder.

NASA VOICE: *(Under Elizabeth.)* T minus ten…nine…eight…seven…six…
    (Elizabeth reluctantly starts to climb down the ladder.)
NASA VOICE: …we have main engine start…four…three…two…one…And lift-off, we have lift-off of the twenty-fifth space shuttle mission. And it has cleared the tower.
    (Elizabeth is standing on the stage now, looking up at her mother.)
ASTRONAUT VOICE: Houston, we have roll program.
NASA VOICE: Roger, roll Challenger. Go with throttle up.
    (Explosion. Elizabeth keeps looking at her mother. The explosion reveals the

birth of a galaxy, as seen through the eye of the Hubble—God's view of a stellar nativity. Elizabeth, fearlessly stretches her hand up to touch it. Blackout.)

END OF PLAY

TATJANA IN COLOR

———◆•◆———

Julia Jordan

This play is *very* loosely based on
events in the life of Egon Schiele.

THE AUTHOR

Julia Jordan received the Francesca Primus Prize and was shortlisted for the Susan Smith Blackburn Award for *Tatjana in Color*. She was a 1994 Playwrighting Fellow and 1995 Playwright in Residence at Juilliard. Ms. Jordan has been commissioned for new works by South Coast Repertory and GeVa Theatre, as well as by Actors Theatre of Louisville for a ten-minute play.

Ms. Jordan's full-length plays include *Smoking Lesson* which was work-shopped at the Sundance Playwrights Lab, and directed by Seret Scott in 1995; The Intiman Theatre New Voices Festival, Seattle in 1995; and The Cleveland Playhouse New Work Festival in 1996.

Tatjana in Color was written at Juilliard and The Playwrights Center in Minneapolis. It was given a work in progress production at the Actors Studio Free Theatre in association with Pure Orange, under the direction of Elizabeth Gottlieb. The play was featured in the Denver Center Theater U.S. West TheatreFest.

Ms. Jordan is currently completing a Master of Philosophy in Creative Writing degree at Trinity College, Dublin.

AUTHOR'S NOTE

I began writing this play during my first year as a playwriting fellow at The Juilliard School. A friend of mine, Jesse Peretz, was looking toward a career as a film director and approached me with the idea of doing the story of Egon Schiele. He gave me a book of prints with brief liner notes on the painter's life. It readily became apparent that I was far more interested in the girl's dilemma than in Schiele's. I couldn't pass up the opportunity with words that the stage provides and film, in popular understanding, neglects. Jesse was gracious enough to send me off on my own to write a play about Tatjana instead of a film about Egon. I thank him from the bottom of my heart.

Thanks also must be given to all actors, directors, and advisors who worked on the script in its many forms. Including Dan Estabrook, Thomas Caruso, Jeff Croiter, Henry Dunn, Red Ramona, Katherine Roth, Marsha Norman, Christopher Durang, Justin Kirk, Angela Bettis, Tatyana Yassukovich, Christy Romano, Brian Dykstra, Jilly Morris, Elizabeth Gottlieb, Elizabeth Timperman, and Sandy Johnson. As well as, The Juilliard School, The Playwrights Center, The Actors Studio Free Theatre, The Francesca Ronnie Primus Foundation, and Denver Center Theater Company.

Winner 1997 Francesca Primus Playwriting Prize,
Denver Center Theatre Company, Donovan Marley, Artistic Director

ORIGINAL PRODUCTION
In connection with the Primus Prize, *Tatjana in Color* was presented in a Public Reading at Denver Center Theatre Company at the 1998 US WEST TheatreFest. Stage directions by Jeffrey Roark, stage manager was Patricia Collins, and Susan Fenichell was director, with the following cast:

TATJANA . . . . Mayhill Fowler
EGON MALER . . . . Dallas Roberts
WALLY . . . . Jennifer Schelter
ANTONIA . . . . Juliet Smith
VON MOSSIG/SCHOOLTEACHER/JUDGE/DOCTOR . . . . William Denis

Tatjana in Color was first presented as a workshop production by The Actors Studio Free Theater, under the management of Pure Orange Productions, with the following creative team: Executive Producer Arthur Penn; Managing Producer Sandi Johnson; Associate Producer Elizabeth Timperman; Director Elizabeth Gottlieb; Set Design Henry Dunn; Costume Design Katherine Roth; Lighting Design Jeff Croiter; Sound Design Red Ramona; Dramaturg Jill Rachel Morris; Properties Karin Bagan, with the following cast:

TATJANA . . . . Angela Bettis
EGON MALER . . . . Justin Kirk
WALLY . . . . Tatyana Yassukovich
ANTONIA . . . . Christy Romano
VON MOSSIG/SCHOOLTEACHER/JUDGE/DOCTOR. . . . . Brian Dykstra

CHARACTERS
TATJANA GEORGETTE ANNA VON MOSSIG: Twelve. Ordinary looking school girl.
EGON MALER: Twenty-two. Thin. Jarringly self confident.
VALERIE ("WALLY") NEUZIL: Thirties. Egon's lover and match in confidence.
ANTONIA VON MOSSIG: Ten. A tag-along.
VON MOSSIG/SCHOOLTEACHER/JUDGE/DOCTOR: Commanding presence.

TIME AND PLACE
1912. The town of Neulengbach, Austria, twenty miles from Vienna.

ACT I
SCENE I

The forest. Egon is standing up center stage with his back to us. He is wearing a black suit, black hat. White dress shirt open at the neck. He holds one arm behind his back and in that hand is an orange. Tatjana and Antonia are downstage left with plaited hair and wearing gray school uniforms. Tatjana and Antonia stare at Egon's back and his orange. Egon kneels down, still with his back to them and us, and rolls the orange slowly downstage and stands. The two girls scramble for it.

Blackout.

SCENE II

Egon as before. The girls as before. Egon doesn't move. The girls wait. Tatjana pushes her sister forward.

TATJANA: You.
> *(Antonia steps back and pushes Tatjana.)*

ANTONIA: No. You.
> *(Tatjana takes a step towards Egon. Then closer. Closer. She reaches out to take the orange. Egon spins around startling her. He gives her the orange.)*
> *(Blackout.)*

SCENE III

Egon is standing in the same place but is facing the girls. His arm is extended offering the orange. Tatjana walks towards the orange. Antonia follows. Tatjana puts out her hand to take the orange. Egon snaps his back. Tatjana and Antonia jump at the sudden movement. Egon extends the orange a second time. Tatjana puts out her hand. Egon snaps his back. Wally appears elegantly dressed in burgundy. Egon smiles at her. Wally walks over and links arms with Egon. They slowly walk stage right with Egon extending the orange to Tatjana behind him. The girls don't move. Wally and Egon pause and look over their shoulders, waiting for Tatjana, offering the orange. Tatjana starts to follow.

ANTONIA: No, Tatjana!

TATJANA: Why, no?

ANTONIA: I will tell father.

TATJANA: Tell father I am in love with oranges!

> (*Antonia grabs Tatjana's arm as she tries to follow. Egon turns around, kneels.*)

EGON: Tatjana.

> (*Egon rolls the orange to Tatjana. He smiles and links arms with Wally and they walk off.*)
>
> (*Blackout.*)

SCENE IV

> *Tatjana is sitting cross-legged on the ground. She is holding two pieces of orange rind over her eyes. Antonia is standing over her.*

ANTONIA: What are you doing?

TATJANA: I am a gypsy.

ANTONIA: You are not. You are Tatjana holding dead fruit to your eyes.

TATJANA: I am a gypsy. I have gypsy blood. And I am divining.

ANTONIA: I don't have any gypsy blood and you are my sister.

TATJANA: We gypsies don't let just anybody into our clan. We are very selective. You have to be able to see things, see what is so before anyone else can see it. See the future.

ANTONIA: Can I try?

TATJANA: It is very difficult.

ANTONIA: I'll try very hard. (*Antonia picks up orange peels and puts them over her eyes. Sits cross-legged exactly like Tatjana.*) I'm looking very hard. I don't see anything yet. (*Beat.*) Nothing. (*Antonia takes the orange peels down.*) What are we looking *for?* Perhaps it would help to know.

TATJANA: The man with the oranges. And his wife.

ANTONIA: She is not his wife.

TATJANA: How do you know?

ANTONIA: I heard father talking. He said she is not his wife.

TATJANA: Then why is she with him?

> (*Antonia holds the orange peels up to her eyes.*)

ANTONIA: He gives her oranges all day long. And sprouts.

TATJANA: Why would he give her sprouts?

ANTONIA: She likes them.

TATJANA: Nobody likes sprouts.

ANTONIA: I can see her chewing them and putting butter on them and peeling off their leaves like a brown green rose.

TATJANA: Nobody likes sprouts but you. Nobody peels them away but you.

ANTONIA: But I saw something. So we can be gypsies together.

TATJANA: Gypsies don't lie. Not to one another. You didn't see anything. You made that up.

ANTONIA: I did. You asked why she would stay with him if she weren't his wife and I looked into the oranges and I thought. And I thought. Why, oranges of course. He has lots of oranges. Oranges taste very good and one would like very much to be with them all the time. And then I saw sprouts, green sprouts floating before my eyes. Which also taste very good and would make one want to stay close. Especially if he had large quantities of butter as well.

TATJANA: Well then. You are a gypsy. Look again and tell me where he lives.

ANTONIA: Father said…Wait. *(Antonia holds the oranges up to her eyes.)* I see…I see a field and the school. Other side of the field across from school. *(Antonia takes the oranges down.)* Can I fly now? I want to fly. A flying gypsy.

(Tatjana lies on her back and lets Antonia lean against her feet. Holding her sister's hands she hoists her in the air.)

TATJANA: Where are you flying to?

ANTONIA: Up. Up and into the blue, blue sky!

SCENE V

Egon's House. Wally walks barefoot into the house. She is naked underneath a silk burgundy robe. Egon kisses her. They begin to make love. Tatjana creeps up to the house. She clutches the sill and peeks in the window.

Blackout.

SCENE VI

A new day. Egon places a sketch in the window and he and Wally go into a back room. Tatjana emerges from her hiding place. She goes to the window to peek in and sees the sketch. It is a drawing of her peering in at them, her hands clutching the sill. Tatjana sees no one inside, so climbs in the window to steal her portrait. She looks around taking in the empty wine bottles, cigarettes and clothing strewn about. She sees the paints and brushes. She has an idea and on another piece of paper, paints an orange undetailed. She places it in the window just as before and runs out with her treasure.

SCENE VII

Tatjana is peering in the window. Wally is posing for Egon. Tatjana attempts to mimic Wally's exact pose. The painting finished for today, Wally undoes her hair. She shakes it out, a mess of wild curls. Tatjana undoes her braids and tries to shake her own into an equally messy state. Wally gets up and walks outdoors in her silk robe for fresh air and a cigarette. She pretends not to see Tatjana who mirrors her every move. The way she sits. The way she pushes her hair behind her ear. The way she strikes a match and lights her cigarette. Tatjana smokes an imaginary one, drag for drag. Wally glances at Tatjana, her mussed hair and her invisible cigarette.

WALLY: Smoke?

TATJANA: No, Ma'am. *(Tatjana drops her hand and her invisible cigarette.)*
 (Wally stares off as if young girls hanging around outside the house while she poses nude for the painter is an ordinary occurrence.)

WALLY: A white sky today, or is it lavender?
 (Egon comes out, shirttails untucked.)

WALLY: I offered her a cigarette. She declined.

EGON: It's oranges she's after I'm afraid. *(Egon sits down next to Tatjana.)* I have no oranges today. None to eat. I do however have pieces of gold.

TATJANA: I don't like money.

EGON: Money is beneath us.
 (Wally laughs to herself. Egon pulls from his pocket a glazed pastry wrapped in a handkerchief.)

EGON: Gold. It will make your belly warm and shine, blinding the sun.
 (Tatjana takes the pastry bites into it immediately.)

EGON: Someday I should like to paint you like that. Shining like that.
 (Wally wipes a crumb from Tatjana's lip.)

WALLY: It's lovely to be painted. Often when I have nothing to do it's my most favorite thing in the world.

EGON: A little secret, just between you and me, I am the greatest painter in the world.

WALLY: Charming isn't he.

EGON: Did you like my picture?

TATJANA: Yes, sir.

EGON: Would you like me to make another one of you?

TATJANA: Yes, sir. But bigger.

WALLY: How do you mean?

TATJANA: Bigger. Like the big ones inside. With lots of colors.

EGON: Of course.

TATJANA: Bigger than me even.

EGON: As big as you. Life size.

TATJANA: Please.

EGON: But you've got to give me something.

TATJANA: I haven't got any money.

EGON: I don't like money.

TATJANA: I don't have anything.

EGON: Give me something to paint.

(Silence.)

WALLY: Take off your clothes.

SCENE VIII

The schoolroom. The Schoolteacher wears a classic black schoolmaster robe. He is lecturing. Antonia sits perfectly attentive, hair neatly braided in her gray schoolgirl skirt and pressed white blouse. Tatjana's hair is still loose and messy, her blouse a little askew. She is not paying attention. She is scribbling.

SCHOOLTEACHER: And so one must eat three square meals of sensible food a day. Unless one is trapped on a boat bound for less enlightened places. A word to the wise. Never Travel. The desire indicates a dissatisfaction which is utterly unbecoming a young lady. But if you should be forced asea, be sure that food containing the proper vitamins is aboard as well. All one needs to do, to see the ravages of an unstable diet, is visit one of those shipyards and observe the ignorant sailors that have allowed themselves to be subjected to scurvy. The country of England, so unfortunately surrounded by the sea, is teeming with shipyards and scurvy sailors. It is often best to avoid England altogether. Limeys altogether.

Called limeys because of their solution, however unsuccessful judging by their relative lack of attractiveness, their solution of eating large quantities of limes on their constant voyaging. They are such an unholy looking race one sometimes wonders if they should even bother...Eating limes. Scurvy or no, they are a sickly looking bunch.

(He begins to stalk towards Tatjana. Antonia tries to distract him.)

ANTONIA: My father is a sailor. A captain!

SCHOOLTEACHER: Tatjana. Miss Tatjana von Mossig. TATJANA.

TATJANA: Yes, Sir.

SCHOOLTEACHER: Tatjana. May I inquire after your hair?

TATJANA: Sir?

SCHOOLTEACHER: Your hair, Tatjana. Your overwhelmingly loose hair.

TATJANA: I ran all the way here. I didn't have time.

SCHOOLTEACHER: All the other girls with nicely plaited hair have been studying vitamins and the importance of a healthy diet. Perhaps you... *(Schoolteacher has approached Tatjana's desk.)* ...would stop your... *(Schoolteacher picks up Tatjana's drawing.)* ...grotesque scrib...IS THAT SUPPOSED TO BE ME?

(Tatjana is deeply offended by the insult to her drawing.)

TATJANA: It's a bowl of fruit! Oranges, which like limes, contain vitamin C.

(Schoolteacher rips Tatjana's drawing in half.)

SCHOOLTEACHER: Vitamin C is an easy one.

ANTONIA: Not for the sailors.

SCHOOLTEACHER: If one can't draw well, one shouldn't draw. Unrecognizable pictures make fools of us all.

(Tatjana stares as the Schoolteacher crumples each half of the paper in each of his fists.)

SCHOOLTEACHER: Art theory concluded. Beriberi is a disease caused by? *(Beat.)* Caused by the deficiency of which vitamin?

(Antonia raises her hand. He ignores her.)

TATJANA: B?

SCHOOLTEACHER: And the symptoms of beriberi? *(Beat.)* The symptoms. The symptoms of beriberi.

TATJANA: I don't know, Sir.

SCHOOLTEACHER: Of course you do. You can sit here and ignore us all. Ignore what we teach. Ignore how we wear our hair! And still! You know which vitamin deficiency causes the disease. Vitamin B! You said so yourself. So speak up! Continue! What are they? What are the symptoms?!

(Antonia nudges her to offer a clue. Tatjana elbows her hard to "back off.")

TATJANA: I'm sorry, Sir.

SCHOOLTEACHER: You don't know what they are or you can't be bothered to respond? Please von Mossig, my patience. My patience. A person struck with beriberi is struck with what symptoms? What symptoms?

(Humbled, Tatjana looks to Antonia who simply ignores her.)

TATJANA: A person struck with beriberi. A person struck with beriberi. Is beriberi sick.

(The sound of schoolgirls dissolving into peals of laughter.)

SCHOOLTEACHER: TATJANA VON MOSSIG! TATJANA GEORGETTE ANNA VON MOSSIG!

(Tatjana runs out. Antonia does her best to look perfect and smiles at the schoolteacher.)

SCENE IX

Egon is sitting on the floor with a spread of coffee for himself, milk for her, sugar and a pastry. Tatjana sits across from him, knees to her chest.

EGON: A little coffee in your milk? *(Egon pours some coffee from his own cup into her milk.)* Sweet? *(He sugars her drink and stirs.)* Drink. It's lovely. *(Tatjana drinks and eats too fast.)*

EGON: Enjoy it. Not so fast. *(Beat.)* You have crumbs and milk on your lips. *(Egon dabs her mouth with the tail of his shirt.)*

TATJANA: Would you like to paint my lips? I'm sure they are shining. *(Beat.)* Or would you like to kiss them?

EGON: No. *(Egon traces the underside of her thigh lightly. Barely touching, if at all.)* This?

(Tatjana is very still, holding her milk. Wally enters and takes off her coat. Egon rises. He goes to his easel and starts to sketch. Wally goes outside to smoke.)

EGON: Finish your milk.

SCENE X

In the forest. Bare white stage. Tatjana has her own easel, paper and pencil. She sets up a still life of fruit. She takes off her scarf and tosses it into her scene. Antonia is sitting on the ground next to the still life playing with a pet mouse. Tatjana moves her easel so Antonia will not be in the picture. She adjusts a piece of fruit, turns her back and returns to the easel. Antonia scrambles to the other side of the arrangement so she is once again in the picture. Tatjana looks up to find to her dismay, Antonia sitting once again in the way stroking her mouse.

SCENE XI

The inside of Egon and Wally's house. Egon is preparing his paints and canvas. As Tatjana takes a drawing out of her schoolbag.

TATJANA: Do you like my picture? *(Tatjana holds up the piece of paper. The drawing is really just a black splotch in the center.)*

EGON: Your lack of interest in quality of line is touching.

TATJANA: Yes, but do you like it?

EGON: I like its violence.

(Tatjana looks at her picture.)

TATJANA: What violence? I don't see violence.

EGON: The man and woman are, shall we say, struggling.

TATJANA: What man and woman? Where?

EGON: There. Her back may be shielding him from view but there is her neck straining towards him.

TATJANA: You know very well there is no man or woman. Only a bowl of fruit and a scarf.

(Egon tries not to laugh.)

EGON: Perhaps that is what you looked at while you drew but, to my eyes, it is not what you have drawn.

TATJANA: Would you prefer a drawing of fruit or a struggle?

EGON: A struggle please.

TATJANA: You may have it. But first, you must give me something.

EGON: I have no money.

TATJANA: I don't like money. I would like to be kissed.

EGON: You, little Tatjana, have too much.

(Egon walks out to gather his paints, he passes Wally on her way in. Wally and Tatjana prepare to pose together.)

TATJANA: Wally?

WALLY: Yes.

TATJANA: Wally, if a boy, or man, should touch me, or you, or any of us, here.

(Tatjana traces the back of her leg.) Lightly, lightly though, ever so lightly. Should we be ashamed to ask him to do it again?

WALLY: Shame? No. Shame would be an excuse for a fearful heart.

TATJANA: And I should not be afraid?

WALLY: Of a boy! Never.

TATJANA: Good. Because I'm not. Just disappointed. It's infuriating. They thump about every which way and never land the way they're supposed to. The way I want them to.

WALLY: They improve. In a few years they will respond quite nicely to your demands.

TATJANA: My father hasn't. He always does and says exactly what I don't want. And he's clumsy. I can't imagine him touching anyone softly just there. *(Tatjana strains to picture it.)*

WALLY: Don't try. Or your pretty little head will be in a mess.

TATJANA: I think it is somewhere between. Neither boy nor father.

WALLY: You are a clever thing.

TATJANA: Somewhere, where Egon lives.

WALLY: For now.

TATJANA: He does. Doesn't he? Touch you there. Whenever you ask? *(Tatjana traces Wally's leg.)*

WALLY: And here, and there and anywhere. *(Wally traces Tatjana's shoulder and then down her nose and then tickles her.)*

TATJANA: And do you have to give him presents first?

WALLY: I don't have to do anything.

TATJANA: And does he kiss you? There? *(Tatjana touches her lips.)*

WALLY: On demand.

TATJANA: And if I asked very kindly, softly, so as not to frighten him, would he kiss me? There?

WALLY: I don't think you are quite big enough yet to frighten Egon.

TATJANA: I'm going to be terrifying. Someday. Now he only buttons me up and kisses my cheek and says, "You were very still. You were very good." And I think to myself, next time, next time I will be stone. For him, I will learn not to breathe. And so I practice and as I grow more still with each sitting I hope for his kiss to fall closer to my mouth. But those awful millimeters are so imperceptible. I am not sure if he is any closer to where I want him to be.

WALLY: Those kisses, the kind you are thinking of, are only for love.

TATJANA: Egon loves you?

WALLY: How could he not?

TATJANA: Then why hasn't he married you?

WALLY: I am not the sort a man marries.

TATJANA: But he does love you and that is enough. Will he love me?

WALLY: You charm him.

TATJANA: Yes but will he love me?

WALLY: What does he tell you?

TATJANA: He says I have too much.

WALLY: You charm him.

TATJANA: Too much what? It isn't talent. I can see. He could still love me without talent couldn't he? You don't have any and he loves you.

WALLY: I have many talents.

TATJANA: But me. What about me?

WALLY: I will love you. Will that be enough?

(Tatjana holds up her drawing for Wally to see.)

TATJANA: Wally? When you look at my drawing what do you see?

WALLY: Hmmm...A girl spinning around so fast the dust flies up from under her feet causing a halo of delight to cover her.

(Tatjana looks at her drawing again.)

TATJANA: That's right.

WALLY: Or, maybe, just a bowl of fruit with a scarf tossed in.

(Egon re-enters. Wally and Tatjana are intertwined. Egon prepares to paint. Tatjana looks at a painting on the wall.)

TATJANA: Who is that? It is not Wally and it is not me.

EGON: My sister. Gerti. Be still.

TATJANA: She's naked!

EGON: My first model. What was I to paint? Arranged fruit?

TATJANA: But your sister, naked before you!

EGON: How, my dear, was I to see her body when swaddled in muslin and wool?

TATJANA: You could have used your imagination. Imagined her body. In your mind.

EGON: Gerti is my sister! For me to imagine her naked body in my mind. That wouldn't be quite correct.

TATJANA: I have seen my sister naked. But I am not a man. And her body is ugly. Scrawny like a boy. Unsuitable for painting. Quite unlike Wally and myself.

WALLY: It is the pastries. They are making you fat.

TATJANA: I am not fat and it is not the pastries. It is the coffee. I think it is the coffee. My father does not allow coffee in my milk. Never sugar. It is the coffee. It makes me hold my head differently. Like a lady.

(Tatjana drinks from Egon's cup in her best imitation of Wally. Wally laughs.)

WALLY: Nearly a lady.

TATJANA: And such a lady I'll be! I will wear nothing but dressing gowns made of burgundy satin, like you. I will always be a mistress. Never a wife. Like you. I will be adored and dismissive but charming in my own fashion. And like you I will be loving and sweet to all the housewives who resent me. I will be just like you.

WALLY: A stunning ambition.

TATJANA: And I will paint better than any man alive like Egon.

EGON: Better than myself?

TATJANA: I'm sorry Egon, but when I am a lady you will be an old man. Decrepit. Barely able to hold a brush.

(Tatjana reaches for a pastry. Egon holds the tray out of her reach.)

EGON: If it is the pastries that have created this monster, they will be furthermore withheld. I believe it is her head that is getting fat. Now. Stillness.

(Wally gets up and lights a cigarette.)

WALLY: Intimidation, my love?

EGON: By her drawings? No. But I have worked tirelessly on my arrogance and perhaps that alone has been challenged. Tatjana, I am twenty-two and in the prime of life. You my insolent one are twelve. When you are twenty-two...

TATJANA: I will be a fine fatale of Vienna.

EGON: I will be only thirty-two...

TATJANA: Excruciatingly fine.

EGON: And still in the prime of life!

WALLY: But perhaps balding a little.

TATJANA: And I will be a woman and you only a man.

EGON: A wife. With one by your side and one on the way.

TATJANA: A mistress! And you a balding man.

EGON: Only thirty-two!

TATJANA: But still just a man. You have no choice. But I can. I can choose not to be what you just described. Can't I Wally?

WALLY: You may.

TATJANA: Then I'll choose to never be a wife. I'll be a mistress. Talked about and cleverly floating among them. Oh, but Egon, now I'm sad. What will keep you young?

EGON: I have my paints.

TATJANA: Yes. You can paint us.

> *(Wally and Tatjana strike poses and make him laugh.)*

EGON: I will paint myself.

TATJANA: I will paint you too. Be you as drearily decrepit as time demands.

EGON: You will paint me?

> *(Tatjana leads Egon to one of his own self portraits.)*

TATJANA: You are an excellent subject, don't you think?

EGON: Excellent. But perhaps, my dear, you are not a painter.

TATJANA: In my mind I am. I have begun to believe that maybe the whole world is really in my head and I can do anything I want with it. Everything I see, touch, paint, smell, taste. Not real at all. My bigger imagination. Everything and all of you. Mine.

WALLY: Tat, if it is so and I am yours, please do something wonderful with me.

TATJANA: Oh, I will.

> *(Egon returns to his painting.)*

EGON: Nothing is yours until it has passed through your mind and out of your hands.

TATJANA: I like it when you say things like that and that is why you say them. I will teach you both how to live in my world and we will live apart from all of them. We will do whatever we want and it will be lovely. So lovely…that sometimes, when we are quiet, we will cry.

SCENE XII

> *Antonia runs on holding her pet mouse Valentino.*

ANTONIA: Mother is very angry. You have not done your chores. There is the kitchen floor to sweep and you are supposed to mend your own torn skirt. Mother says you have grown wild and boyish and she will not mend your rips and tears any longer.

TATJANA: Take off your clothes.

ANTONIA: I will not.

TATJANA: I said take off your clothes and loosen your hair or I will hit you.

ANTONIA: I will not!

TATJANA: Why, why, why?

ANTONIA: I will not be ridiculous.

TATJANA: You are. Petting that mouse. That rodent.

ANTONIA: He is very soft. And my friend.

TATJANA: Well. I do not wish to paint a schoolgirl stroking a fieldmouse. I want to paint the birth of Venus.

ANTONIA: Venus?

TATJANA: But you are afraid of being ridiculous.

ANTONIA: You want me to be Venus?

TATJANA: You will not take off your clothes.

ANTONIA: Do you think I look like Venus?

TATJANA: I will have to place your eyes further apart. And they will have to be green. Not that muddy hazel. Then there are the breasts to deal with. Venus has them. The shell and the sea and that horrid mouse. But you will do.

ANTONIA: I hate you again all over again every moment.

TATJANA: I'm not interested in your expression.

ANTONIA: You are so changed. Why are you this way? Why is your hair sticking straight up to the sky? Why are you always running away from me and saying cruel things to me?

TATJANA: Because you are my little sister.

ANTONIA: Who has done nothing. An innocent. A poor, sweet, good child.

TATJANA: And that is why you are boring.

ANTONIA: I am not. I am the fairy of the forest and Valentino is the sprite that serves me.

TATJANA: Valentino is a mouse.

ANTONIA: He is a sprite with magical powers.

TATJANA: Such as what?

ANTONIA: He can turn you into a toad at my bidding. Or a statue!

(Tatjana poses as a statue.)

TATJANA: I would much rather be a statue.

ANTONIA: It is not what you'd rather. It is what I bid. Anything I bid. I am the fairy of the forest. And all in the forest must do as I bid. I bid you to make a portrait of my majesty holding the sprite Valentino.

TATJANA: Naked.

ANTONIA: You are insufferable and I am going to tell mother. And father! I am going to tell father this instant.

TATJANA: Tell and I will turn the sprite Valentino into the dead carcass of a mouse.

ANTONIA: You wouldn't.

TATJANA: I would. I'd feed him to the cats. I would.

(Antonia picks up her mouse and stalks off. Tatjana looks around considering.)
TATJANA: Landscapes. Always landscapes.

SCENE XIII

Egon's home. Wally and Egon are about to make love. Tatjana runs in out of breath.

EGON: No painting today.

TATJANA: Why no?

EGON: Because sometimes there are better things to do.

TATJANA: I came all this way.

WALLY: She ran all this way.

EGON: Then give her a coffee and something sweet. But by the time it is consumed, I intend to hear your Papa calling you home. You must have chores to do.

TATJANA: Papa's house therefore Papa's chores. You don't do chores and I find your mess so inviting.

(Wally prepares the coffee with Tatjana looking eagerly on.)

WALLY: Occasionally we clean.

TATJANA: Occasionally you throw cluttering things out the window. I have seen the pile. It is not the same as a proper cleaning.

WALLY: Would you have me scrubbing on my hands and knees?

TATJANA: Oh no. Not my Wally. Your knees would callous and that would never do.

EGON: Never! I like her knees soft. And her hands. Her face.

TATJANA: And mine?

EGON: Yes, and yours too. *(Egon starts for the back room.)*

TATJANA: Where are you going?

EGON: To throw cluttering things out the bedroom window. I think Wally and I shall start afresh there after you have returned home to your Papa like a good little girl. *(Egon exits.)*

TATJANA: I'm not a good little girl, and someday everyone will say so.

WALLY: He wouldn't like you so much if you were.

TATJANA: Why is he looking so happy today? Is it because of the kissing?

WALLY: Perhaps, or maybe he's just tired.

TATJANA: What is it like to kiss him?

WALLY: Like this! *(Wally grabs Tatjana playfully and kisses and tickles her.)*

TATJANA: Stop! Stop! That isn't the way.

WALLY: Oh, but it is.

TATJANA: You weren't laughing.

WALLY: I was inside. You just couldn't see it.

TATJANA: Show me how he kisses when he isn't happy. Be his miserable self. Sometimes I think that is how I like him best.

(Wally pours the coffee and spoons in sugar for Tatjana.)

WALLY: Well, let me see…

TATJANA: Draw in your cheeks. Make your skin look like the most fragile membrane. As if to touch would be unbearable. And wonderful! Try to look like you are miserable in the most delightful way possible.

(Wally attempts to follow her directions.)

TATJANA: Egon tries to look like he could die for love. He fails so charmingly.

WALLY: Love of me or love of paint? *(Wally gives Tatjana her pastry.)*

TATJANA: I think I should love to die of a broken heart.

WALLY: And won't it seem ever so glamorous when it actually happens.

(Tatjana starts to take off her jumper.)

WALLY: What are you doing?

TATJANA: I don't like to wear clothes in this house. I don't understand why anyone ever would.

WALLY: Put on your clothes. Go home.

TATJANA: May I wear your robe? Your burgundy satin robe! Please!

(Egon pops his head in from the other room. He sees Tatjana and covers his eyes in mock horror.)

EGON: What is that naked child doing in my house?!!!

TATJANA: I am about to wear satin!

EGON: Well then, while you are slithering around in satin, perhaps you could spare me your companion. For I am growing lonely all alone.

(Wally goes to Egon.)

WALLY: Tatjana, I do think I hear your Papa calling.

TATJANA: I don't.

EGON: Oh, yes. A long way off but quite distinct.

TATJANA: I don't hear a thing. Egon, if you are lonely you should stay here with two companions and coffee. Far better than in there with only one and no pastries.

EGON: I'm not in the mood for pastries. *(Egon draws Wally through the bedroom door.)*

TATJANA: Then neither am I! *(Tatjana pushes away her food.)*

EGON: There he is again. Can you hear?

WALLY: Listen, Tatjana. Listen. Your father is calling you home.
   (They close the door.)
TATJANA: I don't hear anything. *(Tatjana puts on the silk robe and puts on some of Wally's lipstick. She goes to the easel and arranges herself in the most fetching pose she can think of. Then she speaks in a very loud voice.)* I think I should be painted now! I'm glowing now! I'm sure of it! Without the help of pastries.

SCENE XIV

The Forest. Tatjana has talked Antonia down to her underwear. Valentino is in a cage nearby. Tatjana rips up her drawing.

TATJANA: Lie down.

ANTONIA: Why?

TATJANA: Because I am the artist and you are my muse. Lie down.
   (Tatjana throws the crumpled paper on the ground. Antonia scoops it up. Tatjana tries to retrieve it but Antonia jumps out of reach, opens it and looks.)

ANTONIA: That is not me. I look nothing like that!

TATJANA: You will.

ANTONIA: Never.

TATJANA: Oh, yes you will.

ANTONIA: I look like a great cow. A great dairy cow!

TATJANA: Where are the hoofs? I see no hoofs. I drew the hands quite well actually.

ANTONIA: Those! I don't have those! I will never have those huge things hanging off of me. This is not me. This is Aunt Ethel.

TATJANA: You take after Aunt Ethel. Everyone says so.

ANTONIA: They do not. I do not.

TATJANA: Every evening when you have been sent to bed. We all sit around. Mother, Father, Grandmother and I. We all sit around the table and we say, "My, oh my. Antonia grows more like dear old Aunt Ethel every day." And then we sigh sweetly, "Ohhhhhhh."

ANTONIA: Aunt Ethel is a cow.

TATJANA: She is a kind old soul.

ANTONIA: She is a great cow and smells of rancid oil and her hair is always dirty!

TATJANA: I will tell her you said so unless you take off those ridiculous underpants!

ANTONIA: Then you will draw me more horribly still! I think maybe you are not very good at drawing.

TATJANA: I draw what I see.

ANTONIA: You did not see those!

TATJANA: I thought if I drew you as a woman perhaps you might improve.

ANTONIA: You don't love me, anymore.

TATJANA: I try.

ANTONIA: Try harder. I'm getting cold.

TATJANA: What is there to do? It's hopeless.

ANTONIA: It isn't. I will pose for more hours still if you will love me again.

TATJANA: Where is the hope in that. Look at my drawings! If you could inspire just one inch of a beautiful line or shape, I would love you. I would love you to the ends of the earth. And all the way to Vienna. But as it stands my drawings are no more beautiful than the leavings of pigeons. And it's all your fault.

ANTONIA: Why mine?

TATJANA: You should see the drawings, no, the *paintings* I inspire. Egon's paintings are so...I am Egon's muse. Wally and I. Egon's muse. That is I.

ANTONIA: Egon, Egon, Egon. Egon and Wally. Why can't I go with you?

TATJANA: No.

ANTONIA: Perhaps if you let me come with you I could learn how to be a proper muse. I won't say a word I promise. I could learn. I could inspire the drawing that would make you love me.

TATJANA: No.

ANTONIA: Why?

TATJANA: Because you are too young.

ANTONIA: How do you know?

TATJANA: Because you will not take off your underpants. I always take off my underpants for Egon.

ANTONIA: Now you are lying! I'm sure of it!

TATJANA: I eat golden pastries and oranges and sweets. I have coffee in my milk and sugar, lots of it. And I take off my underpants every time!

ANTONIA: That is a lie and I can prove it so!

TATJANA: Try.

ANTONIA: If you were given sweets and pastries you would not be my sister if you did not bring me some. And I know you are my sister.

TATJANA: You were adopted.

ANTONIA: I was not!

TATJANA: How do you know?

ANTONIA: My family resemblance.

TATJANA: To Aunt Ethel the great cow!

ANTONIA: Why haven't you brought me any sweets.

TATJANA: I'm trying to save you from your very large destiny.

ANTONIA: Liar.

TATJANA: Sweets are only given to proper muses that take off their under-clothes.

ANTONIA: Your lies are piling up behind you like bricks set in a loosely plastered wall. It will fall on you. Fall and crush your proud skull and lying mouth.

TATJANA: Ugly thoughts produce ugly drawings.

ANTONIA: I'm here. I'm your muse. I do as you say. I do my best. I hold my hands very still. For hours. I take off my clothes. I shake from cold and pray that father doesn't walk by. I listen to everything you say. Hand higher, higher and I lift it till it hurts. And still you don't love me. I don't like painting. I don't like you anymore and I don't believe he gives you sweets or paints you at all. If I am as ugly as Aunt Ethel, so are you. You are my sister. We are the same.

(Tatjana takes out some candy and eats it in front of Antonia.)

SCENE XV

The schoolroom.

SCHOOLTEACHER: So, here we find ourselves again, minus the elder Von Mossig. May I ask the younger of her whereabouts?

ANTONIA: Tatjana?

SCHOOLTEACHER: Tatjana. Yes. The elder Von Mossig. You are the younger.

ANTONIA: Where is she?

SCHOOLTEACHER: Do we have a pattern of hearing loss, misunderstanding and absentness running in your clan?

ANTONIA: I'm afraid it may be the hearing. I have been yelled at quite loudly these past days. I believe my tympanic membrane may be damaged.

SCHOOLTEACHER: Is that so?

(Antonia shrugs.)

SCHOOLTEACHER: *(Whispers inaudibly.)* Where is your sister?

ANTONIA: Yes. I believe it is so.

SCHOOLTEACHER: *(Approaching Antonia.)* I will raise my voice. WHERE IS YOUR SISTER!

ANTONIA: My hearing has improved.

SCHOOLTEACHER: If you have then registered my question, perhaps you would answer it.

ANTONIA: Tatjana?

SCHOOLTEACHER: Yes! Tatjana. Tatjana. That name is glued inside my head like some insipid song. Tatjana, Tatjana, Tatjana.

ANTONIA: She is at home. Unwell. Caught a chill I think.

SCHOOLTEACHER: The days are warm.

ANTONIA: Yes, but when one is bare all the time…

SCHOOLTEACHER: Bare?

ANTONIA: Yes. Sir. Tatjana…has taken up with limes.

(The schoolteacher awaits an explanation.)

ANTONIA: Tatjana, it seems was so terrified by your description of the English. Their ugliness and their not having enough limes. That when she looked into the mirror. She isn't so pretty as me. That, well, she flew into a panic and decided to eat limes until her hair turned the color of mine. Or at least cured her face of its ills. Was I to stop her? I think not. It is terrible to be Tatjana and have a sister like me with my resemblance to Venus. No my heart went out to her. And I gave her all my pocket money for all the limes she desired. But as we both know, teacher dear, limes are a sour fruit and the eating of them can be quite disagreeable. And Tatjana is given to sweet things. She is a monster for sweetness really. And selfish. Perhaps that is her real dilemma. Her selfishness has begun to show in her appearance.

SCHOOLTEACHER: And just when did she lose her clothes? •

ANTONIA: Well, that's when the chill took hold. Tatjana decided she would not eat what was good for her. No. "TOO SOUR" she proclaimed, and anyway her looks weren't improving at all. But by *applying* the limes she thought…

(Schoolteacher raises an eyebrow.)

ANTONIA: Rubbing them on her face and soon her body. Her body is no more perfectly proportioned, no matter what she may tell you. By doing this she hoped that the limes would ward off the ugliness you stated had overcome the English. I have thought, and this is a secret, that our poor Tatjana was perhaps adopted from that country, England. My father, despairing that I had not yet arrived, maybe stopped during his naval voyages on the shores of England and found her on the doorstep of a shipyard hotel. It could be true! My father doesn't say much one way or the other. So there's no way of knowing. And thus the ugliness and therefore *the limes.* Sitting naked in the night air covered with lime juice, she has caught a chill and so will not be attending school today. Our hearts should go out to her I think. Perhaps a prayer? *(Beat.)* I believe my Aunt Ethel is an English woman too. And no relation of mine.

SCHOOLTEACHER: Thank you for your thoughts, Von Mossig.

ANTONIA: You're welcome.

SCHOOLTEACHER: But I saw Tatjana, quite well this morning, walking in the opposite direction of school.

(Schoolteacher turns his back to return to the head of the class. Tatjana sneaks in hoping she has not yet been missed.)

SCHOOLTEACHER: Today we will discuss the English defection from the church and the matter of a gorging fat English king who could not secure a divorce from his fifth, sixth...? Whichever. One of his wives who he ended up killing anyway so he could delve into the pants of yet another. The Pope quite rightly stated, "Enough is enough." meaning food as well as wives, and that is how the entire country of England reverted to heathendom. Good riddance. Welcome, Tatjana.

TATJANA: Sir.

SCHOOLTEACHER: Educational opportunities afield?

TATJANA: Sir?

SCHOOLTEACHER: Perhaps since you are finished with your education you would like to teach the class.

TATJANA: How do you mean sir?

SCHOOLTEACHER: Teach us something.

TATJANA: Like what, sir?

SCHOOLTEACHER: Something you know and we do not.

(Tatjana looks at the Schoolteacher as if to ask "Really?" Schoolteacher gives a sarcastic "yes" look back to her.)

TATJANA: I have recently learned that the sky is not blue.

SCHOOLTEACHER: Of course it's blue.

TATJANA: It is not. That is only what you told us to color our skies.

SCHOOLTEACHER: And who told you the sky is not blue?

TATJANA: I've seen it. The sky is transparent and cobalt as night draws near. And black and today it is white. It comes in all manners of gray. Periwinkle and orange and red and lavender and purple and gold. The sky is not blue.

SCHOOLTEACHER: You are, both Von Mossigs, liars and dismissed.

SCENE XVI

Egon's house. Wally is outside. Antonia creeps up to the house.

ANTONIA: Hello.

WALLY: Hello.

(Antonia stoops down and picks up a stone.)

ANTONIA: I am collecting stones.

WALLY: I can see.

ANTONIA: To build a cottage.

WALLY: A large ambition.

ANTONIA: For my mouse.

WALLY: A smaller ambition. I'd rather you built one for me.

ANTONIA: But you already have one.

WALLY: It's not mine.

ANTONIA: Are you alone?

WALLY: Is it information you are collecting or stones?

ANTONIA: My sister. Tatjana? do you know her? She tells me you do. But she is full of lies. She is the deceptive one. I am the pretty one. I have this hair you see. Tatjana tells me there are piles of sugar and butter and jam inside. Pastries. And oranges. She tells me you don't wear any clothes. She lies and says that she doesn't wear any either and that that man paints her like that. With no clothes. I don't believe a word of it. And I have not told anyone. Not even Father. I can be trusted not to repeat lies. Is it true you don't wear clothes?

WALLY: I too can be trusted not to repeat. Lies or otherwise. *(Wally goes inside.)*

SCENE XVII

Antonia is standing in her underwear with a pained expression on her face. Tatjana nods at her. She grimaces and begins to take off her underpants. She stops, and decides to take off her undershirt first. She is about to slip it over her head. The sound of schoolgirls laughing. Antonia screams. Tatjana throws rocks, chases them away. Antonia is crying. Tatjana goes to comfort her. Antonia pulls her hair.

TATJANA: OW!

ANTONIA: And I'll do it again. I hate everyone. That lady, Wally. School-teacher. And them. And you. *(Antonia pulls Tatjana's hair again.)*

TATJANA: Ow! *(Tatjana pulls Antonia's hair.)*

ANTONIA: Ow! You are a wayward child.

TATJANA: I'm older than you.

ANTONIA: Mother said you were a wayward child and Father will say so too. You made me take off my clothes!

TATJANA: Look at the drawing. Look how beautiful you are.

ANTONIA: I'm not! Your drawing is ugly and they laughed at me.

TATJANA: You are. Don't tell.

ANTONIA: I will tell. And all this will stop. No more painting. No more fruit. No more sugar and coffee! Nothing!

TATJANA: Think of your mouse. Think of Valentino.

(Antonia quickly gathers up her clothes.)

ANTONIA: You could not be so evil.

TATJANA: I could. I am!

ANTONIA: I don't believe you.

TATJANA: There are a lot of hungry cats in Nuelengbach!

ANTONIA: *I'm telling and you can't stop me.*

(Tatjana slaps Antonia hard. Antonia steels herself.)

ANTONIA: I'm telling.

SCENE XVIII

Egon's house. Tatjana is posing nude. Wally is outside smoking.

EGON: Tatjana, what ever happened to the still girl?

TATJANA: She was not well appreciated. So she has been sent away.

EGON: Conjure her back for me. Just five minutes more.

TATJANA: Only you can bring her back.

EGON: How?

TATJANA: Kiss her into existence. *(Tatjana closes her eyes and holds her mouth up for a kiss.)*

EGON: I have been trying very hard to be good. Couldn't you try as well? To be good and still?

(Tatjana opens her eyes.)

TATJANA: No one is looking.

(Egon steps towards her. He touches her lips with his finger, tracing them.)

EGON: Be still.

TATJANA: That was not a kiss.

EGON: That is a kiss to us. *(Egon traces her knee.)* And here is another and that is all.

(Von Mossig enters the yard. He takes in Wally's presence. Wally is undisturbed.)

WALLY: Smoke?

VON MOSSIG: No.

WALLY: We have no oranges.

VON MOSSIG: Is my daughter here?

WALLY: Blonde?

VON MOSSIG: No.

WALLY: Red?

VON MOSSIG: No.

(Wally holds up her hand indicating the height of six foot three.)

VON MOSSIG: No.

(Wally lowers her hand to the size of a dwarf.)

VON MOSSIG: No.

WALLY: It's hard to tell.

(Inside, Tatjana closes her eyes again and purses her lips disturbing the pose.)

TATJANA: One more?

(Egon grins and dips his brush in blue paint and splatters her.)

EGON: No!

(Tatjana laughs and smears the blue paint all over her face.)

VON MOSSIG: That is her.

WALLY: You are mistaken. That was a blonde laugh. Too high for anything else.

VON MOSSIG: I know my daughter's laugh.

WALLY: You said yourself she is not a blonde.

(Von Mossig brushes by Wally and opens the door on Tatjana posing for Egon.)

EGON: Be still, Tatjana. Still.

(Tatjana sees her father and scrambles to cover herself.)

TATJANA: No.

VON MOSSIG: Come.

TATJANA: No.

VON MOSSIG: I SAID COME!

(Von Mossig grabs Tatjana by the arm and drags her out, knocking over paint brushes and upsetting an easel. Wally stands outside the door and looks in at Egon.)

End Act I

ACT II
SCENE I

Lights up on Antonia holding a string tied to the leg of a dead Valentino. She gives a loud piercing cry.

SCENE II

Egon's cell. Tatjana is somewhere on stage though not physically in the scene. Wally is let in. She carries his suit and a clean white shirt. She has also brought his paints and paper.

WALLY: They agreed. *(Wally gives him her presents.)*

EGON: Idiots.

WALLY: They agreed.

EGON: Not to my innocence.

WALLY: You shouldn't hope. They allowed you your paints. Your clothes.
(Egon inspects his shirt and suit.)

EGON: Such a suit. It is a shame I haven't served. A uniform, some brass or epaulets might be more to their liking. They like uniforms.

WALLY: They would have liked it better had you painted the girl in hers.

EGON: And better still had I painted her father in his. The seacaptain. A study in the grotesque.

WALLY: Remember tomorrow to hold that sort of talk in check.

EGON: I look a tad too fine. They hate my looks. Is the collar too long? I think it may remind them of the city.

WALLY: Perhaps.

EGON: Cut it off. Do you have a knife?

WALLY: I brought one for the fruit. From Tatjana. *(Wally hands Egon the orange and Tatjana's note.)*
(Lights dim. Tatjana steps on stage into her own light to say the letter. Wally cuts off the collar during the reading.)

TATJANA: Dear Egon,
Each time I walk by the patisserie I cry for you. For the shinyness of the pastries now makes me cold like my Father's house. Cold and dying. Your prison cell seems a heaven and me the most wronged for being locked out in this world. I would like to be surrounded by a confinement of gray to match my insides. I curse the sun every morning and the

stars mock me. Flowers are depetaled in my path. And small animals are dying. I know your suffering is above mine and my envy of imprisonment is evil. Jealousy is a terrible disease but evil is now my most favorite word. I have become a murderer and so perhaps my wish is truly fitting. A murderer and the owner of a spiteful, jealous little sister. We must forgive her. Eventually. After a long fretful silence. She only wanted the oranges I think. And still she must be punished. And so, again she is deprived. This orange is for you. Oh, Egon! I am growing thin. Wasting away on my Father's potatoes. But then I see Wally, and though we are not allowed to speak, the sight of her fills me up. I watch her walk away. She walks so well. It is a shame you can't paint a walk. When I am grown and can walk like her I will walk sublimely all the way to Vienna. And us three, Wally, Egon and Tatjana, will continue. Where the pastries are exquisite and the coffee is hot and thick with beans and cream. I can feel my new self inside. Pushing out in all my corners. They can not prevent us when I am new. I think I am in love with my new self and you, —Tatjana.

(Lights out on Tatjana.)

WALLY: What does she say?

EGON: Nothing.

WALLY: Read it to me.

EGON: It is nothing. Schoolgirl musings.

WALLY: Egon?

(Wally hands him the shirt with the collar gone. Egon inspects the collar.)

EGON: The collar will do. I will look like a peasant. Appearances.

WALLY: It would have *appeared* better had we been married.

EGON: That can not be taken care of as easily as the collar.

WALLY: Your chances could still improve if we make plans to marry.

(Egon tries on the shirt.)

EGON: I have just now decided to hate the provinces. Has the fresh country air gotten to your senses? Implanted these visions of home and hearth in your head? You women are so problematic! Whose chances would improve?

WALLY: Both of ours.

EGON: I am the only one on trial.

WALLY: They will call me your whore.

EGON: You have been called worse. *(Egon finishes buttoning his cuffs.)*

WALLY: Do you love me?

EGON: With all my heart.

WALLY: Then marry me for love and appearances.

EGON: When we return to Vienna you will forget this request.

WALLY: If you are convicted we will not return to Vienna. My testimony as your intended could prevent that. They would not believe that a wife could sit by and watch her husband with a young girl. A whore though. A whore, that is another matter.

EGON: They will not convict me. There is nothing to convict me on. But when this is over they will try to relegate me to the pile of personalities. "Ah, there goes Egon Maler. Have you heard about him? They say he is quite adventurous in the matters of sheets and pillows. He paints young girls and he married that woman, you know." My painting cannot be out shone by these things.

WALLY: Then what will you paint? Arranged fruit?

EGON: There are many things to paint.

WALLY: And many cleaner women to marry?

EGON: I promise you, when I marry I will not love her. In our bed I will think only of you.

WALLY: You will marry then.

EGON: A marriage will appease them. In some things I must learn to abide. Look around you. This belongs to them and I am inside it. Here I sit accused of stealing that child's soul, when it is I who gave her one.

WALLY: Like you gave me mine?

EGON: You will stay with me. Even if I marry.

WALLY: You never gave me anything. Surely not yourself.

EGON: I paint you. Your soul will shine down from my canvases into the eyes of people born long after we're gone.

WALLY: They are only pictures. And if anyone should look at them long after we're gone, and pause to reflect upon my soul, all they will think, is that maybe you painted me again and again because I had one. You did not give it to me, and your pictures could not capture it but you will take it away.

EGON: Where will I take it, Wally?

WALLY: Into the wedding bed of another. You will trade it for paint.

EGON: What will you tell them?

WALLY: The truth.

SCENE III

The forest. Antonia plaits Tatjana's hair.

ANTONIA: Is it too tight?

(Tatjana sits stonily, no words. She is obviously resigning herself to her former appearance under her father's command and much duress. Antonia pulls harder making Tatjana wince. Still Tatjana will not speak, even to tell Antonia to stop hurting her. Antonia starts to cry but does not let Tatjana see. Antonia pulls Tatjana's hair harder still. Trying to yank it out by the roots. Tatjana bears it without flinching or making a sound.)

SCENE IV

The courtroom. The Judge is in a uniform of black robes and serves as examiner. Egon wears his black suit. Wally is dressed extravagantly in bright colors and scarves. Tatjana and Antonia are in their gray school uniforms with plaited hair. Antonia enters and sits on the stand. She tries to catch Tatjana's eye. Tatjana will not look at her.

JUDGE: Antonia. Come here dear. Are you scared?

ANTONIA: No. I am the innocent.

JUDGE: Tell us what happened when Tatjana began visiting this man's house.

ANTONIA: I only wanted to be not so much alone. That is all. She grew so happy. The larger her smile the more mine squished with sourness. I did not want to tell tales. Even if they were true. It is very difficult. Very difficult.

JUDGE: Tell me a tale. A true one. Tell me about Tatjana. What was she like before she met this man?

ANTONIA: She was herself. Now Tatjana doesn't understand. She doesn't even try. Like I do. I try so hard.

JUDGE: What do you have to understand?

ANTONIA: Why my sister is a MURDERER!

TATJANA: It was the cat.

ANTONIA: You tied him to the chair!

(Tatjana stands and hold out her hands to be tied.)

TATJANA: I am an accomplice only. To that I confess. You may put me in jail if the tomcat will come along as well. I will join Egon immediately.

JUDGE: Sit down Tatjana.

ANTONIA: She should go to jail. She should. I am the good sister. She is the bad.

JUDGE: But she wasn't always bad. Was she?

ANTONIA: It was lurking.

JUDGE: What do you mean?

ANTONIA: Now when I think back I can see. Oh yes! She was bad from the beginning. She would do things. And say things. She is the tale teller.

JUDGE: And since she met this man, Egon, what tales did she tell?

ANTONIA: Horrible ones.

JUDGE: About?

ANTONIA: Cats.

JUDGE: Did Tatjana ever take you with her? To Egon's house?

ANTONIA: She is too selfish.

JUDGE: What was she keeping all to herself?

ANTONIA: Sweets. And she is not allowed to eat so many! It is against the rules! She said I was too young.

JUDGE: To young for candy?

ANTONIA: No! Because I would not take off my underpants.

JUDGE: Why, in order to visit the house, did you have to take them off?

ANTONIA: To make pictures. Haven't you ever seen the birth of Venus?

JUDGE: Yes. But I've also seen many pictures of beautiful girls with their underpants on.

ANTONIA: But Venus is the most beautiful. That's how she got to be Venus.

JUDGE: Thank you for reminding me.

ANTONIA: Now may I remind you that Valentino is dead?

JUDGE: I remember. Now tell me clearly. Was there any other reason why you had to take off your clothes, other than the pictures, if you wanted to visit the house of Egon Maler and eat all those nice candies?

ANTONIA: No.

JUDGE: Are you sure? Don't you know of any bad thing Egon Maler did to Tatjana? Something we should punish *him* for?

ANTONIA: OF COURSE! He stole her away and turned her into a murderer! That is what I'm trying to tell you! Why doesn't anybody understand? An old man should not steal away a young girl's sister. It isn't kind. He already has a friend. Some one his own age to play with. Why should he have two and leave me with none? Little me, all alone, with nothing and no one. No friends and no sweets. Only a mouse and now he is gone too. That was a very bad thing to do Herr Egon! Very bad. Both of you are. When people grow up they do very bad things. They steal people away.

They steal little animals away. They make you take off your clothes. And they do not share their candy! I hope to never grow up. Never be like you. You are...All of you...Terrible. At night, I dream in my bed alone. I dream that the whole world is wiped clean of all of you. And of all cats And only I am left. Just me and the mice. Hundreds of them. I am the queen of the mice and we are very happy. They feast on cheese. I give them all the cheese that is. And I build each one a cottage with a grass roof. Each mouse alone. They each live alone and do not go around making pairs to vex me. A cottage and a round of cheese. That is all that they would want and they would have it. I would give it to them so we could waste no more time and just spend the days playing. Just play and stroke soft fur and poke our pink noses where they don't belong. No traps waiting for us and no cats. No rules. No one telling us to come home and go to bed. That is what I dream. And I dream it comes true without any of you. You are not invited. You can all stay here. (*Antonia returns to her seat.*)

JUDGE: Thank you, Antonia. Valerie Neuzil.

(*Wally takes her place.*)

JUDGE: You were present at the meeting of Von Mossig's daughter and Egon Maler.

WALLY: I was.

JUDGE: You were present during the painting.

WALLY: I was.

JUDGE: You were aware of the girl's youth.

WALLY: I was.

JUDGE: How were these painting done? Tell us.

WALLY: I cannot.

JUDGE: You were there.

WALLY: I was.

JUDGE: Then speak on it.

WALLY: I cannot.

JUDGE: Your lips move. Sound flows forth. It resembles words.

WALLY: I cannot speak of painting. I am not a painter. My talents lie elsewhere.

JUDGE: Tell us of your talents then.

WALLY: They also lie amongst the unspeakable.

JUDGE: You are an unmarried woman.

WALLY: I am.

JUDGE: Led astray.

WALLY: You can tell by my disposition that I am not one to walk with a lead.

JUDGE: You have lived openly with this man. There is evidence of your arrangement. The paintings are in my chamber.

WALLY: You have enjoyed them I suspect. Behind closed chamber doors.

JUDGE: Miss Neuzil. There is a least one heartbroken little girl present. Doesn't that give you pause?

WALLY: Yes.

JUDGE: Then tell us simply how it came to be that Von Mossig's daughter lay naked before your lover?

WALLY: I helped her to undress.

JUDGE: Why would you do that? Are you not still a woman? Is it possible that you felt no maternal allegiance to someone so much younger and more innocent than yourself?

WALLY: I helped her. I let her wear my robe when it was done. Girls. All little girls like to try on women's clothes. Love to take off the old and put on the new. A brighter color. A softer velvet. A deeper cut. That they find themselves naked between the changes is unavoidable.

JUDGE: And when they are naked, what happens?

WALLY: Many things.

JUDGE: Such as? You didn't purposely send this man's innocent daughter down your own path out of spite, did you? Are you an accomplice?

(Wally is still.)

WALLY: To what crime?

JUDGE: Touching a child.

(Wally is still.)

JUDGE: Tell us the truth. You were present always. You saw everything.

WALLY: He painted her. She was willing. I was present.

JUDGE: If that is all, sit down.

(Wally walks to her seat.)

JUDGE: Tatjana Georgette Anna Von Mossig.

(Tatjana approaches. There is the loud sound of whispers. She takes her place.)

TATJANA: Yes, sir?

JUDGE: How did it come to be that you were discovered in the presence of this man without your clothes?

TATJANA: I took them off.

JUDGE: How did that happen?

TATJANA: Buttons were unbuttoned, sashes undone, laces untied. With these things completed clothes take a notion to fall away. But all women do things without their clothing. Why, bathe for one. And only a few years ago it mattered not who saw me without them. And only a few years from now it will again matter not. For my Father won't even know. Father is very angry because I will keep my hands as soft as Egon's and Wally's. That is the real reason this has come about. The real reason Father is angry is because I was eating gold with Egon when I was supposed to be doing Father's chores. But I will not sweep or mend his clothes for him any longer. And I will never be a wife who does so. Work. Work is for other people. Not for people like us. Egon, Wally and I. We are special. Touched. Feel my hands. *(Tatjana holds out her hands.)* They are soft. And will stay as soft. Father and all of you are merely angered not to be one of us. Father's hands are rough and callused. But I, I have been touched. I have a soul. Egon told me that.

JUDGE: And we who work? We do not?

TATJANA: I used to think you did. But now that you have taken him away from me, I think, perhaps, your souls are only in my mind. Not real at all.

(The Judge turns to Egon.)

JUDGE: She says we do not. Maler, your pit of depravity widens. I cannot help but notice how very black it is in there.

EGON: That is why I always carry with me a light.

(Egon takes the orange from his pocket and smiles at Tatjana. Tatjana returns the conspiracy.)

JUDGE: What did he do? Did he give you something in exchange? Exchange for your lack of clothing?

TATJANA: Gold!

JUDGE: You them took off for money?

TATJANA: We don't like money. Not money. No. Gold. He offered me gold. Pastries with marmalade glaze to make them shinier still than butter alone. They made me shine and then he made me beautiful. He traced my leg in the blackest way. It was lovely.

JUDGE: Black?

TATJANA: Charcoal and ink.

JUDGE: But did he touch you?

TATJANA: Yes. Right here. *(Tatjana places her hand on her chest.)* On my heart and deep inside. We ate gold. Didn't we Egon? Didn't we Wally? Creams and coffee and gold!

JUDGE: He put his hands on your body?

TATJANA: He arranged me.

JUDGE: With his hands.

TATJANA: Oh, yes. Higher. Higher with your arm. Move there. Here. Lower your face. Just like that.

JUDGE: And you would do what ever he said?

TATJANA: Anything.

JUDGE: So he told you to take off all of your clothes and then…

TATJANA: No. I often left my socks. Egon liked it very much when I kept my socks on. Only my socks. I thought he found my feet ugly. But he said it was just the opposite and he liked the color of my stockings. I have a pair of blue ones, that come up very high, of which he is particularly fond. I also have a pair of green and of course my gray and…

JUDGE: Miss Tatjana I am not interested in stockings.

TATJANA: Wally said all men were interested in stockings.

JUDGE: *I am not interested in clothing of any sort. If you had been clothed I would not be interested. I am only and exclusively interested in the parts of you that were unclothed!*

ANTONIA: I don't know why you are talking about stockings when Valentino is dead! Is murder not a crime?

JUDGE: Be still, Antonia.

TATJANA: I have confessed. I am an accomplice to murder! Lock me away with Egon and I shall attain a higher heaven than any of you could hope to aspire to!

JUDGE: Tatjana!

ANTONIA: Tell them how he died!

JUDGE: QUIET!

ANTONIA: An accomplice? No. MURDERER!

JUDGE: *QUIET!!!*

TATJANA: A hungry cat often finds himself a mouse. That's the way of cats.

JUDGE: I DEMAND QUIET!

ANTONIA: Tied to a chair! She tied a piece of twine around his pink foot and tied him to a chair! It was not fair!

TATJANA: You cannot hope for fairness when you are a mouse. You are too small! Things are not fair!

JUDGE: STOP THIS! *(Beat.)* Where is your shame? Has he taken that too?

TATJANA: It felt good to hurt something smaller than me. I have a deciding mind. You decide to take Egon. You decide to take Wally and her colors. Well so do I. I decide to take a little life away too.

JUDGE: *Of the paintings!* Are you not ashamed of the paintings? We have all seen your nakedness!

TATJANA: I have not taken off my clothes for any of you.

JUDGE: There is no need. We have the paintings. Your father, Tatjana. Your Father has seen them. We have sat together staring at them. Breasts and legs. You are not so much a child. How does that make you feel to know that we looked?

TATJANA: I don't know.

JUDGE: What would cause you the requisite shame? Shall we hang them in the bedrooms of old men who pay high prices. Then might you know how to feel? For that is where they were intended. Or in the streets for the young boys. Those boys do love a good laugh. Maybe that would be more effective. What shall we do my girl to make you more appropriate? What shall we do to make you to cry?

TATJANA: I will not cry.

JUDGE: Maler.

(Egon rises, straightens his shirt cuffs and walks to the stand.)

JUDGE: You live unmarried with this woman Valerie Neuzil. You buy her food and clothing in return for this arrangement. Do you deny it?

EGON: I do not.

JUDGE: Previous to meeting you I trust she did not reside in certain, less dignified sections of Vienna. This arrangement was not her trade. Do you deny her life as such began with you?

EGON: I do not.

JUDGE: And likewise you began with the young Tatjana Von Mossig by providing her with the sugars that young mouths crave. Do you deny it?

EGON: I do not.

JUDGE: And so led her astray. Previous to encountering you I am told she had no penchant for destroying fieldmice, she attended school regularly, was obedient to her Papa and was generally untroublesome. Do you deny it?

EGON: I have no knowledge of her before she encountered myself. That would be hearsay.

JUDGE: You Viennese. You cultivate sass in Vienna, don't you. Quite a crop of it this year I understand. But out here in Neulengbach the more of it that is imported the more its currency has a tendency to plummet. Do not make light of this. The paintings sir. The paintings are unflinching. Anatomical. She was exposed!

EGON: She is lovely.

JUDGE: You have no right to say so. Or think so. She is not yours.

EGON: All that I see is mine to paint. There is, I believe, no law against painting.

JUDGE: Against this sort there is. This is not painting. This is corruption. An innocent girl no longer so. And the men who pay you your pretty prices. Financial gain, sir. Cold money passed over her prostrate body, from the hands of sweaty Viennese into your silk lined pockets. Why should we believe you stopped there. What evidence is there you did not hold her down and take more?

EGON: I did not.

JUDGE: Her naked body stood before you! And you did not?

EGON: I did not.

JUDGE: Are you asking us to believe that it is possible to paint such pictures and *not?*

EGON: I demand you do.

JUDGE: You are in no position to make demands. DID YOU OR DID YOU NOT TAKE VON MOSSIG'S DAUGHTER'S CHILDHOOD?

EGON: I did not. I only painted it in color.

JUDGE: The paintings bear witness that she is no longer truly a child. And too young to be anything else. Of her corruption you are guilty. I hope to never look upon such a thing again.

EGON: I think that is not quite true.

JUDGE: What did you say?

EGON: You have seen younger than Tatjana painted with winged backs flying on the ceilings of your country church. It is at them you gaze while listening to sermons against gazing. You think you are staring at the heavens while your sight is bouncing off the ceiling and back into your earthbound lives.

JUDGE: But this is not an angel of your imagination. She is a live girl. I have a daughter of my own. This is Von Mossig's daughter. His.

EGON: I do not believe you, sir. I do not believe you have passed through this life and not looked upon the body of a young live girl. A sister, my judge? A daughter. A child you don't know swimming alone, unaware she is watched. Tell me otherwise. I will not believe. But these are treasures. I am your treasure that allows you to look. Look longer. Allows you not to blink or turn away. You are the criminals to deny me.

JUDGE: The paintings are erotic.

EGON: Only if you see them so.

JUDGE: That is how you saw her.

EGON: She was just a model to me. Nothing more.

TATJANA: Wally?

WALLY: Shhh, Tat…

TATJANA: No! That is not true, Egon. You love me.

JUDGE: Ah. Maler. Have you *loved* her?

EGON: No.

TATJANA: He loves me. I know it.

JUDGE: How do you know? Did he do anything to you that he called love?

TATJANA: He painted me. He made me feel something different. It was love.

JUDGE: You took off your clothes for him. Did he ever take off his for you?

TATJANA: No, not for me. He does not love me as much as Wally. But Egon, you lie. You do love me a little. Wally tell them! That is why I took off my clothes.

SCENE V

The forest. Tatjana and Antonia are sitting on the ground.

ANTONIA: I have been quite bad. This morning I did something terrible. Do you want to know what it was? *(Beat.)* I will undoubtably be punished severely. *(Beat.)* I'll tell you if you like. You can even tell Papa. I won't mind so much. *(Beat.)* When Papa was in his bath, I took from his pocket two coins. One for you and one for me. And I ran away. I ran all the way to the sweet shop in town and I bought two chocolates. See? In the shape of diamonds. And inside of each is a surprise of almonds. One for you. And one for me. Here. Take yours.

(Antonia offers the chocolate. Tatjana will not respond.)

ANTONIA: Take them both. *(Antonia offers both.)* I cannot eat. Soon he will discover his missing coins. And soon after discover me. And then we will both have been spanked. Punishment always makes me lose my appetite. Perhaps if Papa had a chocolate he would not be so angry. Perhaps we should feed Papa chocolates all day long and he would grow fat and content and the shiny buttons of his uniform would burst and go bouncing off the walls! And we would have no more trouble with Papa. I think I will save one chocolate for him. The other is yours. I will go without.

(Antonia picks up Tatjana's limp hand and puts the chocolate in her sister's palm and curls the fingers around it.)

(Tatjana lets the chocolate drop.)

ANTONIA: Would you like to draw? I will take off all my clothes. I don't care!

(Antonia starts to take off her blouse.)

(Egon appears in his traveling clothes. Tatjana grabs Antonia and buttons her up. She stands shielding Antonia from Egon's view.)

TATJANA: *(To Egon.)* Go away.

EGON: I'm sorry.

(Tatjana gives Antonia a push to leave. Antonia stops, opens Tatjana's hand

and puts the chocolate in it. As if to say, "Only if you accept this will I leave, will I not tell." Tatjana takes it. Antonia exits. Tatjana turns back to Egon.)

EGON: I must leave for Vienna. Wally is nearly ready.

TATJANA: In Vienna there are others to paint. Prettier than me and without fathers. Lots of them. You will be very happy.

EGON: I'm sorry.

TATJANA: Will you paint them?

EGON: I don't make a practice of painting fruit.

TATJANA: I don't care who you paint. When I am grown I will find you in Vienna. Then you will paint me. Only me.

EGON: When your hair is pinned and not plaited. When your Father no longer knows quite who you are.

TATJANA: You won't take me with you?

EGON: A kidnapping charge? Prison doesn't suit me. Twenty eight days. It was enough.

TATJANA: Will you paint me when you are gone. Paint me from your mind. So when I find you I can watch my changes? Could you remember me like that? Changing?

EGON: Give me something to remember you by.

TATJANA: I haven't got any money.

EGON: We don't like money.

TATJANA: If you would teach me how to kiss, I could kiss you goodbye.

(Tatjana offers Egon the chocolate. Egon smiles and reaches out to take it. Tatjana snaps it back and smiles. She gives it to him, closes her eyes and turns her face up for a kiss.)

EGON: Open your eyes.

(Tatjana opens her eyes and Egon kisses her on the mouth. The kiss continues. Wally appears to collect Egon. She is holding her packed suitcase. Moments pass as Wally passes through changes acknowledging the situation. A slight movement on Wally's part attracts Tatjana's attention away from Egon. Wally and Tatjana look at each other. Egon notices Tatjana staring over his shoulder and turns to see Wally standing there. Egon leaves them alone.)

TATJANA: You are not married.

WALLY: No. I'm not.

(Wally takes off her burgundy scarf and drapes it around Tatjana's neck in the same fashion in which she wore it. Wally unpins her own hair. She takes Tatjana's braids, twists and pins them up. She gives to Tatjana her traveling coat and case. Tatjana is transformed into her eighteen year old self newly arrived in Vienna.)

SCENE VI

This scene should melt out of the previous. Six years later in Vienna. A museum.

TATJANA: Wally...

WALLY: I once thought, not too long ago, that no one would ever leave me. Not me. Or rather, that I would never mind if they did. It is still an amazement that he managed it.

TATJANA: Why hasn't he come to see me?

WALLY: I also thought I would never want children. I still don't. Though I wouldn't mind having a daughter, I suppose. Something like you.

TATJANA: Why hasn't he come to see me? I've waited six years

WALLY: How old are you now?

TATJANA: Eighteen.

WALLY: Eighteen?

TATJANA: He is here in Vienna. Isn't he?

WALLY: Your small sister. With the pretty hair. How old is she?

TATJANA: Sixteen.

WALLY: Has she a new mouse?

TATJANA: She has outgrown pets. Wally?

WALLY: Tatjana. Grown. And Egon, I wonder if they have a painting of his here. Probably. They are everywhere. His wife sits for him now. Neatly. Upright in a chair, top button tightly buttoned, skirts to the floor. It is a good thing really. I hear she has horrendous legs. He is probably balding. As you predicted. You, Tatjana, you have come true. Who will paint you now?

TATJANA: Haven't you heard me?

WALLY: He paints wealthy men in uniforms now. And suits. I suppose he likes the money.

TATJANA: You used to answer all my questions. Answer me now.

WALLY: I gather you have come to stay. You will miss your sister.

TATJANA: I locked her in the closet so she couldn't follow.

(Antonia stands in the doorway holding a bag with clothing spilling out of it. Her hair is mussed. She holds a letter triumphantly in her hand.)

WALLY: She got out.

(Tatjana turns and sees Antonia. They stalk towards each other.)

ANTONIA: *I found her letter.*

(Wally walks over to them and gets between them and puts a hand on each chest, lightly holding them back from attacking.)

TATJANA: *How far must I go to leave you behind?*

ANTONIA: I'm your sister and Vienna is only twenty miles from home.

TATJANA: Wally, you have to tell me. I need to be with him. And far away from *her!*

WALLY: He can't see you.

TATJANA: But I'm here. In Vienna. I'm grown.

WALLY: I can see. But he won't see you.

TATJANA: Wally, did he love me?

WALLY: He liked to paint you.

TATJANA: Yes, but did he love me?

WALLY: Sometimes when they are of her, I think I see your eyes peeking out from under her lids.

TATJANA: ANSWER ME!

WALLY: Not as much as I did. Do you understand? *(Beat.)* What have you done these past years?

TATJANA: Held my breath.

(She touches Tatjana's face.)

WALLY: Tatjana Georgette Anna Von Mossig, are you a painter?

TATJANA: I have no talent.

WALLY: That is not such a terrible thing.

(Wally steps away from Tatjana and Antonia takes her place.)

TATJANA: In Neulengbach, I pulled your hair. I said terrible things. I pushed you in the closet and I locked it.

ANTONIA: We, neither of us, like small places.

TATJANA: *Why are you here?*

ANTONIA: It is clear you are not an artist, or you would understand that WE ARTISTS must follow our muse. And I knew you'd miss me.

TATJANA: Wally, take me with you!

(Tatjana looks for Wally and sees that she is gone. Antonia waits.)

TATJANA: So…here we two are, in Vienna.

(Antonia takes from her pocket a pastel and starts to draw around Tatjana a perfect orange circle. [On a blank hanging canvas.])

ANTONIA: Yes! Have you seen the sky? *(She colors in the orange as the lights fade.)*
(Lights out.)

END OF PLAY

THE HOUSE OF
BERNARDA ALBA

Federico Garcia Lorca
Adapted in English by Emily Mann

THE AUTHOR

Emily Mann is in her eighth season as Artictic Director of McCarter Theatre. Ms. Mann wrote and directed *Having Our Say: The Delany Sisters' First 100 Years,* which had its world premiere at McCarter Theatre prior to its successful run on Broadway and its national tour. For *Having Our Say,* Ms. Mann received the Hull-Warriner Award, two Joseph Jefferson Awards, as well as Tony, Outer Critics and Drama Desk award nominations. Her McCarter directing credits include the world premiere of Richard Greenberg's *Safe As Houses* (Feb. 1998), *Betrayal, The Mai, A Doll House, The Perfectionist, Miss Julie* (also adapted), *Cat on a Hot Tin Roof, Three Sisters, Betsey Brown* (co-author), *The Glass Menagerie, The Matchmaker* and *Twilight: Los Angeles, 1992.* She also wrote *Greensboro (A Requiem)* which had its world premiere at McCarter in 1996. Ms. Mann made her Broadway debut as playwright and director with *Execution of Justice,* for which she received numerous awards including a Bay Area Theatre Critics Award, a Playwriting Award from the Women's Committee of the Dramatists Guild, a Burns Mantle Yearbook Best Play Citation, and a Drama Desk nomination. Her play, *Still Life,* premiered at the Goodman Theatre and opened off-Broadway at the American Place Theatre under her direction in 1981, winning six Obie awards, including Distinguished Playwriting, Distinguished Directing and Outstanding Production of the Season. Her first play, *Annulla, An Autobiography,* premiered at the Guthrie Theater and was produced at The New Theatre of Brooklyn with Linda Hunt. Ms. Mann is a member of the Dramatists Guild and serves on its council.

Emily Mann would like to thank Dana Harrell and Mara Isaacs for their literal translation and Janice Paran for her dramaturgical support.

ORIGINAL PRODUCTION

The House of Bernarda Alba was originally produced at the McCarter Theatre, October–November, 1997, directed by Emily Mann with the following cast:

BERNARDA ALBA	Helen Carey
MARIA JOSEFA	Lucille Patton
ANGUSTIAS	Molly Regan
MAGDALENA	Tracy Sallows
AMELIA	Annika Peterson
MARTIRIO	Natacha Roi
ADELA	Gretchen Cleevely
A MAID	Giulia Pagano
LA PONCIA	Isa Thomas
PRUDENCIA	Tanny McDonald

CHARACTERS

BERNARDA: (age 60)
MARIA JOSEFA: Bernarda's mother (age 80)
ANGUSTIAS: Bernarda's daughter (age 39)
MAGDALENA: Bernarda's daughter (age 30)
AMELIA: Bernarda's daughter (age 27)
MARTIRIO: Bernarda's daughter (age 24)
ADELA: Bernarda's daughter (age 20)
A MAID: (age 50)
LA PONCIA: a maid (age 60)
PRUDENCIA: (age 50)
A BEGGAR WOMAN AND CHILD (non-speaking)
* WOMEN IN MOURNING (non-speaking)

*In Mann's production there were twenty women.

SETTING

In Emily Mann's production, the entire play took place in the courtyard of
Bernarda Alba's house.

NOTE: Most of the stage directions appear as they do in Lorca's original text.
The writer states that the play is intended as a photographic document.

ACT I

It is summer. A great brooding silence fills the stage. It is empty when the curtain rises. Bells can be heard tolling outside.

MAID: *(Entering.)* The sound of those bells hits me right between the eyes.

PONCIA: *(She enters, eating bread and sausage.)* They've been mumbling away for over two hours. The church looks beautiful...When they sang the first response for the dead, Magdalena fainted.

MAID: She's the one left most alone.

PONCIA: She's the only one her father loved. *(She eats.)*

MAID: If Bernarda sees you...

PONCIA: Since she's not eating today, she'd like us all to die of starvation. The old tyrant! Well, I'll fool her. I came back to open a jar of sausages.

MAID: Poncia, can I have some for my little girl?

PONCIA: Help yourself and take a fistful of beans while you're at it. She won't notice the difference today.

MARIA JOSEFA: *(Voice off.)* Bernarda!

PONCIA: Is the old lady locked in?

MAID: Double locked. I put the bar down. She can pick a lock.

MARIA JOSEFA: *(Voice off.)* Bernarda!

PONCIA: *(Yelling.)* She's coming! *(To the Maid.)* Make sure everything's spotless. If Bernarda doesn't see it shine, she'll pull out the few hairs I've got left in my head.

MAID: That woman!

PONCIA: Tyrant over everyone around her. She is capable of sitting on your heart and watching you die for a whole year without taking that cold smile off her wicked face. "Scrub, scrub those floors!"

MAID: My hands are bloody from all the scrubbing.

PONCIA: Oh she's the cleanest, the most decent, she's superior to us all. Her poor husband earned a good rest.

(The bells stop.)

MAID: Are there enough chairs?

PONCIA: Plenty. Let them sit on the floor. She doesn't like people under her roof anyway. Nobody's been to this house since her father died. She's mean.

MAID: With you, she behaves well.

PONCIA: Thirty years washing her sheets; thirty years eating her leftovers; nights watching over her when she had a cough; whole days peeking through a crack in the shutters to spy on the neighbors and tell her the tale; life without secrets one from the other. Curse her. May the nails of the cross pierce both her eyes.

MAID: Poncia!

PONCIA: But I'm a good dog. I bark when I'm told to, and I bite the beggars' heels when she sics me on them. My boys may work in her fields—but the day will come when I've had enough.

MAID: And then…?

PONCIA: And then I'll lock myself in a room with her and spit in her face—for a whole year. "Here's for this, Bernarda, and here's for that, and here's for the other" till I leave her like a lizard the boys have squashed. Because that's what she is—her and her whole family. Not that I envy her her life. Stuck with five girls, fiv ugly daughters—all of them poor—except the eldest, Angustias, by   first husband, she's got some money; but the rest…oh plenty of em   idered lace and linen tablecloths, but bread and grapes is all they'll inherit.

MAID: I'd like to have what they've got!

PONCIA: (At the table.) This glass has some spots on it.

MAID: Nothing will clean it off.

(The bells toll.)

PONCIA: The last prayer for the dead, I'm going over to listen. There is nobody like the old Sacristan, Tronchafinos. At my mother's mass, God rest her soul, the walls shook, and when he sang the Amen, it was like a wolf had come into the church. (Imitates.) A-a-a-a-me-e-en!! (She starts coughing.)

MAID: Watch out, you'll pulverize your throat.

PONCIA: I'd rather pulverize something else.

(Goes out laughing. The maid scrubs. The bells toll.)

MAID: (Imitating the bells.) Dong, dong, dong. May God forgive you! Dong, dong, dong. May you wait many years for me.

(At the door with a little girl, a Beggar Woman with her hand out, murmurs "Blessed be God"…)

MAID: The door to the street's right behind you. Any scraps today are mine.

(Beggar Woman enters, shoves the child in to beg on her knees.)

MAID: Get out! Out! Who said you could come in here? Tracking your filthy feet over my clean floor! Get out! Get out! Out! Out! Out! Get out!

(The Beggar Woman and the Little Girl leave. The maid goes on scrubbing.)

MAID: Linen tablecloths and cupboards while we eat off dirt floors with one plate and one spoon. I pray for the day when not one of us is left to speak of it. *(Bells.)* Yes, ring away! Let them lift you in a silk-lined coffin with gold handles—you're no less dead than I will be. To hell with you, Antonio Maria Benavides, lying there stiff in your wool suit and your tall boots: take what's coming to you! You won't be lifting my skirts anymore behind the barn door! *(Laughs.)*

(Doors open. Two by two, two hundred women in mourning with large shawls and black skirts and fans, begin to enter.)

MAID: Ay! Antonio Maria Benavides, you will never see these walls, you will never break bread under this roof again! I was the one who loved you most of all who served you! *(Pulling her hair.)* Must I go on living after you're gone? Must I go on living?

(Two hundred women stop. Enter Bernarda and her five daughters. Bernarda leans on her cane.)

BERNARDA: *(Screams to the Maid.)* Silence!

MAID: *(Crying.)* Bernarda!

BERNARDA: Less wailing and more work. You should have had all this clean by now. Get out. You don't belong here.

(The maid exits, crying.)

BERNARDA: The poor are like animals: they're made of different stuff.

PRUDENCIA: *(Indirectly.)* The poor feel their sorrows too.

BERNARDA: But they forget them soon enough over a plate of beans. *(To all.)* Sit down.

(Magdalena cries.)

BERNARDA: Magdalena, don't cry. If you want to cry, go do it under your bed. Did you hear me?

(Long pause.)

PRUDENCIA: I haven't felt heat like this in years.

(Long Pause. They all fan themselves.)

BERNARDA: Is the lemonade ready?

PONCIA: Yes, Bernarda. *(She gets a tray of little white jars.)*

BERNARDA: Give the men some.

PONCIA: They're already drinking, in the yard.

BERNARDA: Let them out the way they came. I don't want them tracking through here.

(Awkward Pause.)

PRUDENCIA: *(To Angustias.)* Pepe el Romano was with the men during the mass, Angustias.

ANGUSTIAS: Yes, he was there.

BERNARDA: His mother was there. She saw his mother. Neither she nor I saw Pepe.

(Women buzz.)

BERNARDA: Women in church must not look at a man, unless it is the priest, and only then because he's wearing a skirt. If you turn your head, it means you're itching for the touch of corduroy.

(Women buzz again.)

PONCIA: *(Between her teeth to the women.)* Twisted old vine…itching for the heat of a man!

BERNARDA: *(Beats with her cane on the floor once.)* Blessed be God!

ALL: *(Crossing themselves.)* Bless Him and praise Him forever!

BERNARDA: Rest in peace, with the souls of the departed watching over you…

ALL: Rest in peace!

BERNARDA: With the Archangel Michael and his sword of justice…

ALL: Rest in peace!

BERNARDA: With the key that opens and the hand that locks…

ALL: Rest in peace!

BERNARDA: With the most blessed saints, and the little lights of the field…

ALL: Rest in peace!

BERNARDA: With our holy charity, and with all souls on land and on sea…

ALL: Rest in peace!

BERNARDA: Grant rest to your servant Antonio Maria Benavides, and crown him with your sacred glory.

ALL: Amen.

BERNARDA: *(She rises and chants.)* Requiem aeternam dona eis, Domine.

ALL: *(Standing and chanting in the Gregorian fashion.)* Et lux perpetua luceat eis. *(They cross themselves. They start filing out.)*

PONCIA: *(She enters, carrying a moneybag.)* From the men—money for the mass.

BERNARDA: Thank them, give them some brandy.

(A Young Woman hugs Magdalena.)

BERNARDA: *(To Magdalena, who is starting to cry.)* Ssh!

(She beats with her cane on the floor. All the women have gone out.)

BERNARDA: *(To the women who have just left.)* Go on back to your caves and criticize everything you've seen! And I hope it'll be many years before you pass through my door again!

PONCIA: You've got nothing to complain about. The whole village came.

BERNARDA: Yes, to fill my house with the sweat from their underclothes and the poison of their tongues.

AMELIA: Mother, don't talk like that!

BERNARDA: What other way can I talk about this damned village, a village without a river, a village full of wells, so every time you drink the water you're afraid it's been poisoned.

PONCIA: Look what they did to the floor! *(Poncia cleans the floor.)*

BERNARDA: Like a herd of goats had tracked through here. Give me a fan, child. *(She gives her a round fan with green and red flowers.)*

ADELA: Take this one.

BERNARDA: Is that the fan you give a widow? *(Throwing the fan on the floor.)* Give me a black one and learn to respect your father's memory.

MARTIRIO: Take mine.

BERNARDA: What about you?

MARTIRIO: I'm not hot.

BERNARDA: Well, look for another one, you'll need it. For the eight years we'll be in mourning, not even the wind from the street will enter this house. That's how it was in my father's house and in my grandfather's house. Pretend we bricked up all the doors and windows. In the meantime, you will start sewing your trousseaus. There are twenty bolts of linen in the chest from which to cut sheets and coverlets. Magdalena can embroider them.

MAGDALENA: It makes no difference to me.

ADELA: *(Sour.)* If you don't want to embroider ours, yours will look better.

MAGDALENA: Neither mine nor yours. I know I'm never going to get married. I'd rather carry sacks to the mill. Anything rather than sit in these dark rooms day after day.

BERNARDA: That's what a woman does.

MAGDALENA: Damn women!

BERNARDA: In this house you will do as I tell you. You can't run telling tales to your father now. Needle and thread for the woman, whip and mule for the man. That's how it is for people born to certain obligations. *(Adela goes out.)*

MARIA JOSEFA: *(Voice off.)* Bernarda! Let me out!

BERNARDA: *(Calling.)* Let her out now! *(The maid enters.)*

MAID: I could barely hold her down. She may be eighty years old, but your mother's as strong as an oak tree.

BERNARDA: It runs in the family. My grandmother was the same.

MAID: Several times during the wake, I had to put a sack in her mouth. She wanted to shout out to you to let her have some dishwater to drink and some dog meat. That's what she says you feed her.

MARTIRIO: She's wicked.

BERNARDA: *(To Maid.)* Let her get some fresh air in the yard.

MAID: She took all her rings out of her trunk and her amethyst earrings, put them on, and told me she wants to get married.

(The daughters laugh.)

BERNARDA: Stay with her. Be careful she doesn't go near the well.

MAID: You don't have to worry she'll throw herself in.

BERNARDA: I don't…that's where the neighbors can see from their window.

(The maid leaves.)

MARTIRIO: We're going to change our clothes.

BERNARDA: *(Pause.)* All right.

(Adela enters.)

BERNARDA: And Angustias?

ADELA: *(Meaningfully.)* I saw her peering through the crack in the back door. The men have just left.

BERNARDA: What were you doing at the back door?

ADELA: I went to see if the hens had laid.

BERNARDA: But the men had already left?

ADELA: *(Meaningfully.)* A group of them were still standing around outside.

BERNARDA: *(Furiously.)* Angustias! Angustias!

ANGUSTIAS: *(Entering.)* Do you want something?

BERNARDA: What, or rather at whom, were you looking?

ANGUSTIAS: Nobody.

BERNARDA: Do you think it's decent for a woman of your class to throw herself at a man the day of her father's funeral? Answer me! Who were you looking at?

(Pause.)

ANGUSTIAS: I…

BERNARDA: You!

ANGUSTIAS: Nobody.

BERNARDA: *(Goes forward with her cane.)* You spineless…! Sickening slut! *(She strikes her.)*

PONCIA: *(Running towards her.)* Bernarda!

(She holds her. Angustias cries.)

BERNARDA: Get out, all of you!

(They all go out.)

PONCIA: She didn't realize what she was doing. Of course, I was shocked to see her sneaking off to the back door, and later she stood at the window, listening to the men's conversation. As usual, it wasn't the kind of conversation one should listen to.

BERNARDA: That is why they come to funerals. *(With curiosity.)* What were they talking about?

PONCIA: About Paca la Roseta. Last night they tied her husband up in a stall, threw her over the back of a horse and carried her off to the highest part of the olive grove.

BERNARDA: So what did she do?

PONCIA: She? She was willing. They say she was showing her breasts, and Maximiliano played her like a guitar. It was terrible.

BERNARDA: Then what happened?

PONCIA: What had to happen. They came back almost at dawn. Paca La Roseta had her hair loose, a crown of flowers on her head.

BERNARDA: She's the only bad woman we have in the village.

PONCIA: Because she's not from here. And the men who were with her are the sons of outsiders too. The men from here are not capable of that.

BERNARDA: No, but they like to watch, talk about it, suck their fingers over it.

PONCIA: They were saying other things, too.

BERNARDA: *(Looking from side to side.)* Such as?

PONCIA: I'm embarrassed to say.

BERNARDA: And Angustias heard them?

PONCIA: Of course.

BERNARDA: That one takes after her aunts, all innocent and flirtatious, making big sheep's eyes at the first nobody who pays her a compliment. Oh, what you have to put up with, the fight you have to wage to make them behave decently and not run wild.

PONCIA: It's just that your girls are at an age when they should have husbands. They don't give you any trouble. Angustias must be well over thirty by now.

BERNARDA: She's thirty-nine to be precise.

PONCIA: Imagine. And she's never had a sweetheart…

BERNARDA: *(Furious.)* No, none of them have had a sweetheart, and they don't miss them. They get along very well.

PONCIA: I didn't mean to offend you.

BERNARDA: There's no one good enough to come near them for a hundred miles around. The men in this town are not of their class. Do you want me to turn them over to the first farm hand I see?

PONCIA: You should have moved to another town.

BERNARDA: Oh, I see. To sell them.

PONCIA: No, Bernarda. A change…Of course, in any other place they'd be the poor ones.

BERNARDA: Stop tormenting me!

PONCIA: No one can talk to you. Do we or do we not confide in each other?

BERNARDA: We do not. You serve me, I pay you. Nothing more.

MAID: *(Entering.)* Don Arturo is here. He's come to see about the will.

BERNARDA: Let's go. *(To the Maid.)* You start sweeping out the yard. *(To Poncia.)* And you start putting the dead man's clothes away in the big chest.

PONCIA: We could give some things away.

BERNARDA: Nothing! Not even a button! Not even the handkerchief we covered his face with!

(She goes out slowly, leaning on her cane. At the door she turns to look at her two servants. They go out. She leaves. Amelia and Martirio enter.)

AMELIA: Did you take your medicine?

MARTIRIO: For all the good it'll do me.

AMELIA: But you took it.

MARTIRIO: I do things without believing in them. But like clockwork.

AMELIA: Since the new doctor came, you're much livelier.

MARTIRIO: I feel the same.

AMELIA: Did you notice? Adelaida wasn't at the funeral.

MARTIRIO: I know. Her fiancé won't let her go out, not even to the front door. She used to be happy; now she doesn't even powder her face.

AMELIA: These days you don't know if it's better to have a fiancé or not.

MARTIRIO: It doesn't matter.

AMELIA: It's the fault of that harpy who won't let us live. Adelaida is going to have a terrible time.

MARTIRIO: Do you know how afraid she is of Mother?

AMELIA: What?

MARTIRIO: Because Mother's the only one who knows how her father got his land.

AMELIA: What do you mean?

MARTIRIO: Adelaida's father killed his first wife's husband so he could marry her himself.

AMELIA: *(Whispers.)* My God!

MARTIRIO: Then he left her and went off with another woman who had a daughter, and later he had an affair with the daughter!

AMELIA: Adelaida's mother?

MARTIRIO: Yes. And married *her* after the second wife died insane.

AMELIA: Why isn't a man like that put in jail?

MARTIRIO: Because men help each other and cover up for each other so no one is able to tell on them.

AMELIA: But none of this is Adelaida's fault.

MARTIRIO: No, but history repeats itself. It's better never to look at a man. I've been afraid of them since I was a little girl. I used to watch them in the corral, yoking the bullocks, lifting the sacks of grain, with their loud voices and heavy boots…and always I was afraid of getting older for fear that I would suddenly find myself…in their arms. God made me weak and ugly and kept them away from me.

AMELIA: You can't say that. Enrique Humanes was after you and you liked him.

MARTIRIO: That's only what people thought! One time I stood in my night-gown at the window until daybreak, because he sent the field hand's little girl to tell me he'd be coming, and he didn't come. It was all talk. Then he married someone else, with more than me.

AMELIA: And ugly as the day is long.

MARTIRIO: What do men care about ugliness? All that matters to them is land, yokes of oxen, and a submissive bitch who'll give them something to eat.

AMELIA: Shh!

(Magdalena enters.)

MAGDALENA: What are you doing?

MARTIRIO: Sitting here.

AMELIA: What about you?

MAGDALENA: I've been going through the rooms for the exercise and to look at the needlepoint pictures Grandmother made; the little woolly dog, and the black man wrestling the lion—we liked them so much when we were children. That was a happier time. A wedding lasted ten days and vicious tongues weren't in style. Today, it's more proper. Brides wear white veils just like in the cities and we drink wine from bottles, but we're rotting away inside these walls because we're afraid of what people might say.

AMELIA: Your shoelace is untied.

MAGDALENA: What of it?

AMELIA: You'll trip on it and fall.

MAGDALENA: Well, that'll be one less.

MARTIRIO: Where's Adela?

MAGDALENA: She put on the green dress she made to wear for her birthday, and went out into the yard, shouting, "Chickens, chickens, look at me!" I had to laugh.

AMELIA: If Mother had seen her!

MAGDALENA: Poor thing! Because she's the youngest, she still has dreams. I'd give anything to see her happy.

(Pause. Angustias crosses the stage, carrying towels.)

ANGUSTIAS: What time is it?

MAGDALENA: Well it must be twelve.

ANGUSTIAS: That late?

AMELIA: It's about to strike.

(*Angustias goes out.*)

MAGDALENA: *(Meaningfully.)* Do you know about it yet? *(Pointing to Angustias, with intent.)*

AMELIA: No.

MAGDALENA: Come on.

MARTIRIO: I don't know what you're talking about...

MAGDALENA: You both know better than I, always with your heads together like two little sheep, not letting anyone in on things. About Pepe el Romano!

MARTIRIO: Ah!

MAGDALENA: *(Mocking her.)* Ah! The whole village is talking about it. Pepe el Romano is going to marry Angustias. He was lurking around the house last night and I think he's going to send a declaration soon.

MARTIRIO: I'm glad. He's a good man.

AMELIA: So am I. Angustias has good qualities.

MAGDALENA: Neither one of you is glad.

MARTIRIO: Magdalena! Please!

MAGDALENA: If he were coming because of her looks, for Angustias as a woman, I'd be glad. But he's coming for her money. Even though Angustias is our sister, we're her family and we all know that she's old and sick and has always been the least attractive one of us all. If she looked like a scarecrow when she was twenty; what does she look like now she's nearly forty!

MARTIRIO: Don't talk like that. Good fortune comes to the one who least expects it.

AMELIA: But Magdalena's right! Angustias has all her own father's money; she's the only rich one in this house. And that's why, now that our father's dead and all his money's going to be divided, they're coming after her.

MAGDALENA: Pepe el Romano is twenty-five and the best looking man in this village. The natural thing would be for him to go after you, Amelia, or Adela who's twenty, not the least likely person in the house, a woman who—just like her father—talks through her nose.

MARTIRIO: Maybe he likes it.

MAGDALENA: I've never been able to stomach your hypocrisy.

MARTIRIO: Oh, God!

(Adela enters, in her green dress.)

MAGDALENA: Did the chickens see your dress?

ADELA: What do you want me to do?

AMELIA: If mother sees you she'll tear your hair out.

ADELA: I had such hopes for this dress. I was going to wear it when we went to eat melons by the water wheel. There wouldn't have been another one like it.

MARTIRIO: It's a lovely dress.

ADELA: And it looks good on me. It's the best Magdalena's ever cut.

MAGDALENA: And the chickens? What did they say to you?

ADELA: They presented me with a few fleas that bit my legs.

(They all laugh.)

MARTIRIO: You could dye it black.

MAGDALENA: The best thing you can do is give it to Angustias for her wedding to Pepe el Romano.

ADELA: *(With hidden emotion.)* But Pepe el Romano…

AMELIA: Haven't you heard?

ADELA: No.

MAGDALENA: Well, now you know.

ADELA: But that's not possible…

MAGDALENA: Money makes anything possible.

ADELA: Is that why she went out after the wake, why she was standing at the door? *(Pause.)* And that man would be capable of…

MAGDALENA: …anything.

(Pause.)

MARTIRIO: What are you thinking, Adela?

ADELA: I'm thinking this period of mourning has caught me at the worst possible moment.

MAGDALENA: You'll get used to it.

ADELA: *(Bursting out, crying with rage.)* No, I will not get used to it. I can't stay locked up. I don't want to shrivel up like you, I don't want to lose the whiteness of my skin in these rooms. Tomorrow I am going to put on my green dress and go walking in the street. I want to go out!

(The maid enters.)

MAGDALENA: *(With authority.)* Adela!

MAID: Poor thing, she misses her father. *(The maid exits.)*

MARTIRIO: Quiet.

AMELIA: What happens to one of us happens to all of us.

(Adela calms herself.)

MAGDALENA: The maid almost heard you.

(The maid enters again.)

MAID: Pepe el Romano is coming down the street.

(Amelia, Martirio and Magdalena run hurriedly.)

MAGDALENA: Let's go see him!

(They leave rapidly.)

MAID: *(To Adela.)* Not going?

ADELA: It doesn't make any difference to me.

MAID: He has to come around the corner, you can see best from the window in your room.

(The Servant goes out. Adela is left on the stage, standing doubtfully; after a moment, she also leaves rapidly, going toward her room. Bernarda and La Poncia come in.)

BERNARDA: Curse this…parceling-out.

PONCIA: There's a lot of money for Angustias.

BERNARDA: Yes.

PONCIA: A whole lot less for the others.

BERNARDA: You've said that to me three times, when you know I do not want it even mentioned. "Much less, a whole lot less." Don't remind me of it ever again.

(Angustias comes in, her face heavily made up.)

BERNARDA: Angustias!

ANGUSTIAS: Mother.

BERNARDA: You dare paint your face the day of your father's funeral!

ANGUSTIAS: He was not my father. My father died a long time ago. Have you forgotten?

BERNARDA: You owe more to this man, to your sisters' father, than to your own. Thanks to him, your fortune is increased.

ANGUSTIAS: We'll have to see about that.

BERNARDA: Out of decency. To show respect!

ANGUSTIAS: Let me go out, mother.

BERNARDA: Go out?

MARIA JOSEFA: *(Off stage.)* Bernarda!

BERNARDA: After you have taken all this powder off your face. You…you weakling! You painted whore!

MARIA JOSEFA: *(Off stage.)* Let me out, Bernarda!

BERNARDA: Exactly like your aunts! *(Bernarda violently removes the powder with her handkerchief.)*

PONCIA: Bernarda, don't be such a tyrant!

BERNARDA: My mother may be crazy but I still have my wits and I know exactly what I'm doing.

(They all enter.)

MAGDALENA: What's going on?

BERNARDA: Nothing is 'going on'.

MAGDALENA: *(To Angustias.)* Well if you're arguing about the will—you're the richest—you can keep it all.

ANGUSTIAS: Keep your tongue where it belongs, in your purse.

BERNARDA: *(Beating on the floor.)* Do not think you can get the better of me. Until I am carried out of this house feet first, I will give the orders around here, for all of us!

(Voices are heard and Maria Josefa, Bernarda's mother, enters. She is very old and has decked out her head and breast with flowers.)

MARIA JOSEFA: Bernarda, where is my mantilla? Nothing I own will go to any of you. Not my rings, not my black moiré dress. Because none of you will ever get married. Not one of you! Bernarda, give me my pearl necklace.

BERNARDA: *(To the Maid.)* Why did you let her in here?

MAID: She got away from me.

MARIA JOSEFA: Yes, I got away because I want to get married. I want to marry a real man from the shores of the sea, since all the men around here run away from women.

BERNARDA: Silence, Mother.

MARIA JOSEFA: No, I won't be silent. I don't want to look at these old maids burning to be married, turning their hearts to dust. I want to go home to my village, Bernarda. I want a man to get married to and be happy with.

BERNARDA: Lock her up!

MARIA JOSEFA: Let me go out, Bernarda!

(The maid seizes Maria Josefa.)

BERNARDA: Help her, all of you!

(The daughters grab her.)

MARIA JOSEFA: I want to get away from here, Bernarda! Get married! By the shores of the sea! Down by the shores of the sea. Down by the shores of the sea.

(Quick curtain.)

End of Act I

ACT II

Bernarda's daughters are seated on low chairs, sewing. Magdalena is embroidering. La Poncia is with them.

ANGUSTIAS: I cut the third sheet.

MARTIRIO: That one goes to Amelia.

MAGDALENA: Angustias, should I put Pepe's initials on that one, too?

ANGUSTIAS: *(Dry.)* No.

MAGDALENA: *(Calling, from off stage to Adela.)* Adela, aren't you coming?

AMELIA: She's probably stretched out on her bed.

PONCIA: There's something wrong with that one. She's restless, shaky, she looks frightened—as if she had a lizard between her breasts.

MARTIRIO: There's nothing more or less wrong with her than there is with the rest of us.

MAGDALENA: All except Angustias.

ANGUSTIAS: I feel fine, and anyone who doesn't like it can drop dead.

MAGDALENA: *(Sarcastic.)* Let's admit it. Your best features are your figure and your tact.

ANGUSTIAS: Fortunately I will soon be out of this hell.

MAGDALENA: Maybe you won't get out.

MARTIRIO: Stop it!

ANGUSTIAS: Anyway, better to have gold in your purse than beautiful eyes in your face.

MAGDALENA: This is going in one ear and out the other.

AMELIA: I wish there were a breath of air.

MARTIRIO: Last night, I couldn't sleep because of the heat.

AMELIA: Me either.

MAGDALENA: I got up to cool off. There was a dark storm cloud and a few drops of rain fell.

PONCIA: At one o'clock in the morning, the heat was rising up out of the ground. I got up, too. Angustias was still with Pepe at the window.

MAGDALENA: So late? What time did he go?

ANGUSTIAS: Magdalena, why ask if you saw him?

AMELIA: He left about half past one.

ANGUSTIAS: Oh yes? And how would you know?

AMELIA: I heard him cough and the sound of his horse's hooves.

PONCIA: But I felt he left about four.

ANGUSTIAS: It wasn't him.

PONCIA: I'm sure it was.

MARTIRIO: It seemed that way to me too.

MAGDALENA: Well, that's strange.

(Pause.)

PONCIA: Angustias, come here, tell us, what did Pepe say to you the first time he came to your window?

ANGUSTIAS: Nothing. What should he have said? Just conversation.

MARTIRIO: It's very strange for two people who don't know each other to suddenly meet at a window and get engaged.

ANGUSTIAS: Well, I didn't find it strange.

AMELIA: I would have felt a little...I don't know.

ANGUSTIAS: No, because, when a man comes to a window he already knows from all those people coming and going, going and coming, that she will say "Yes."

MARTIRIO: But he had to say it to you.

ANGUSTIAS: Well of course!

AMELIA: (With curiosity.) And how did he say it?

ANGUSTIAS: Well, it was nothing—just "You know I'm after you: I need a good woman, modest, and that's you if you're in agreement."

AMELIA: Those things embarrass me.

ANGUSTIAS: Me too, but you have to go through with them.

PONCIA: Did he say anything else?

ANGUSTIAS: Yes, he was the one who did all the talking.

MARTIRIO: And you?

ANGUSTIAS: I couldn't have. I felt as if my heart was coming out of my mouth. It was the first time I'd ever been alone at night with a man.

MAGDALENA: And such a handsome one at that!

ANGUSTIAS: He's not bad.

PONCIA: It's easier for people who've had a little experience, who've been taught how to speak and know what to say. When my husband, Evaristo the Birdman, first came to my window...Hahaha.

MARTIRIO: What happened?

PONCIA: It was very dark. I saw him coming closer and when he arrived, he said to me: "Good evening." "Good evening," I said to him and we didn't speak for more than half an hour. The sweat was running down my entire body. And then—Evaristo came closer and closer as if he was trying to squeeze through the bars and said in a very low voice, "Come here, I want to feel you!"

(They all laugh. Amelia gets up, runs and looks through the door.)

AMELIA: Ay, I thought mother was coming!

MAGDALENA: What she would have done to us!

(They go on laughing.)

PONCIA: And then after—he behaved himself. Instead of going to someone else, he started breeding canaries until he died. All of you are single, but you may as well know that fifteen days after the wedding, the man leaves the bed for the table and then the table for the tavern, and any woman who doesn't accept this, rots away crying in the corner.

AMELIA: You didn't accept it.

PONCIA: I could handle him.

MARTIRIO: Is it true you hit him sometimes?

PONCIA: I did: Once, I nearly put out one of his eyes.

MAGDALENA: That's how women should be.

PONCIA: I'm from the same school as your mother. One day, he said something or other to me—I can't remember what—and I killed all his canaries—with a hammer.

(They laugh.)

MAGDALENA: Oh, Adela, you shouldn't miss this!

AMELIA: Adela!

(Pause.)

MAGDALENA: I'm going to go see. *(She goes out.)*

PONCIA: That child is sick.

MARTIRIO: Of course she is, she hardly sleeps.

PONCIA: What *does* she do?

MARTIRIO: How would I know what she does?

PONCIA: You'd know better than me, since you sleep with just a wall between you.

ANGUSTIAS: Envy is eating her up.

AMELIA: Don't exaggerate.

ANGUSTIAS: I can see it in her eyes. She's getting to look like a madwoman.

MARTIRIO: Don't talk about mad women here. This is the one place you shouldn't talk about that.

(Magdalena and Adela enter.)

MAGDALENA: Didn't you say she was asleep?

ADELA: My whole body aches.

MARTIRIO: Didn't you sleep well last night?

ADELA: Yes.

MARTIRIO: *(With intention.)* Well then?

ADELA: *(With force.)* Leave me alone! Asleep or awake it's none of your business. It's my body and I'll do what I want with it.

MARTIRIO: I was concerned about you.

ADELA: Concerned, or nosy. Weren't you all sewing? Well, continue! I wish I was invisible so I could pass through a room without people asking me where I'm going all the time.

MAID: *(Entering.)* Bernarda's calling for you. The man with the lace is here.

(All but Adela and La Poncia go out, and as Martirio leaves, she looks fixedly at Adela.)

ADELA: Stop looking at me. If you want, I'll give you my eyes, they're brighter than yours and my straight back to replace your hump. Just turn the other way when I go by!

PONCIA: Adela, she's your sister and the one who loves you the most.

ADELA: She follows me everywhere. She sneaks in my room sometimes to see if I'm sleeping. She won't let me breathe. And always: "What a shame about the face...What a shame about the body...it won't belong to anyone." But that's not going to happen. My body will belong to whoever I want.

PONCIA: *(With intention and in a low voice.)* To Pepe el Romano. Is that right?

ADELA: *(Startled.)* What did you say?

PONCIA: You heard, Adela.

ADELA: You shut your mouth!

PONCIA: *(In a loud voice.)* Do you think I haven't noticed?

ADELA: Lower your voice.

PONCIA: Kill those thoughts.

ADELA: What do you know about it?

PONCIA: We old women can see through walls. Where do you go when you get up at night?

ADELA: I wish you were blind!

PONCIA: When it's about what this is about, my head and both my hands are full of eyes. I want to know what you're planning. Why did you stand half-naked at the window with the light on the second night Pepe came to talk to your sister?

ADELA: That's not true!

PONCIA: Don't be a child. Leave your sister in peace! If you love Pepe el Romano, hold it in.

(Adela begins to cry.)

PONCIA: Besides, who says you can't marry him? Your sister Angustias is sickly. She won't survive her first birth. She's narrow in the hips, old, and in my experience I can tell you, she'll die. And then Pepe will do what many widowers around here do, he'll marry the youngest, and the prettiest, and that's you. Feed that hope, or forget about him, whatever you want, but don't go against the law of God!

ADELA: Shut your mouth!

PONCIA: I will not shut my mouth.

ADELA: Mind your own business. You sneak! Traitor!

PONCIA: I'll be your shadow.

ADELA: Instead of cleaning the house and going to bed to pray for your dead, you root around like an old sow drooling over other people's affairs.

PONCIA: I keep watch so people won't spit when they pass our door.

ADELA: Why have you suddenly developed this great affection for my sister?

PONCIA: I feel no affection for any of you. But I want to live in a decent house. I don't want to be disgraced in my old age.

ADELA: Your advice is useless. It's too late. I wouldn't just walk over you, you're only a servant, I'd walk over my mother to put out the fire that's running through my legs and burning in my mouth. What could you say about me? That I lock myself in my room and don't open the door? That I don't sleep? I'm quicker than you. See if you can catch the rabbit with your bare hands.

PONCIA: Don't defy me Adela, don't you defy me. Because I can shout, light the lamps, and make the bells ring.

ADELA: You can mount four thousand bright yellow flares on the walls of this house. No one can stop what has to happen.

PONCIA: You want that man so much?

ADELA: So much! When I look into his eyes it's like I am slowly drinking his blood.

PONCIA: I can't hear you.

ADELA: Oh, but you'll have to. I used to be afraid of you. But I'm stronger than you now.

(Angustias enters.)

ANGUSTIAS: Always arguing.

PONCIA: Of course. She wants me, in all this heat, to go and get her I don't know what from the store.

ANGUSTIAS: Did you get me that perfume?

PONCIA: The most expensive one and the face powder. I put them on the table in your room.

(Angustias goes out.)

ADELA: And keep it shut!

PONCIA: We'll see.

(Magdalena, Martirio and Amelia enter.)

MAGDALENA: Did you see the lace?

AMELIA: The pieces for Angustias' wedding sheets are beautiful.

ADELA: *(To Martirio, who is carrying some lace.)* And these?

MARTIRIO: Mine, for a nightgown.

ADELA: Well, it takes a sense of humor.

MARTIRIO: For me to look at. I don't have to flaunt myself in front of anyone.

PONCIA: Nobody sees you in a nightgown.

MARTIRIO: *(With intention, looking at Adela.)* Sometimes...But I love under-clothes. If I was rich I'd have it all made from Dutch linen, all imported from Holland. It's one of the few pleasures I've got.

PONCIA: This lace would be nice for babies' caps and christening gowns. I couldn't afford it for mine. Maybe Angustias will use it for hers. When she starts having babies, you'll be sewing morning and night.

MAGDALENA: I don't plan to sew a stitch.

AMELIA: Much less take care of someone else's children. Look at how our neighbors sacrifice themselves for those four little brats.

PONCIA: They're better off than you. At least they laugh and you can hear them fighting.

MARTIRIO: Go and work for them.

PONCIA: No. Fate has sent me to this convent.

(The bells are heard.)

MAGDALENA: That's the men going back to work.

PONCIA: It's three o'clock.

MARTIRIO: In this heat!

ADELA: *(Sitting down.)* Ay. If only we could go to the fields too!

MAGDALENA: *(Sitting down.)* Each class has its own work.

MARTIRIO: *(Sitting down.)* That's how it is.

AMELIA: *(Sitting down.)* Ay!

PONCIA: There's nothing like being in the fields this time of year. The reapers arrived yesterday morning. Forty or fifty handsome young men.

MAGDALENA: Where are they from this year?

PONCIA: From far, far away. From the mountains. Happy! Like poplar trees! Shouting and throwing stones! Last night a woman arrived dressed in spangles and danced to an accordion. Fifteen of them paid her to go to the olive grove with them. I watched—from far off. The one who made the deal was a young man with green eyes, hard and tightly packed as a sheaf of wheat.

AMELIA: Really?

ADELA: It's possible.

PONCIA: A few years ago another of these women came to the village and I gave my oldest son the money myself so he could go with her. Men need these things.

ADELA: They're forgiven everything.

AMELIA: To be born a woman is the worst punishment.

MAGDALENA: Not even our eyes belong to us.

(A distant song is heard, coming nearer.)

PONCIA: Here they come.

(Tambourines and carranacas are heard. Pause. They all listen in the silence cut by the sun.)

REAPERS: Here come the reapers
    In search of the grain
    Reaping the hearts
    of the women they claim.

MARTIRIO: They don't care about the blazing sun!

ADELA: I wish I was a reaper, to come and go as I please. Then I could forget what's eating us alive.

MARTIRIO: What do you have to forget?

ADELA: Everyone has something.

MARTIRIO: *(Profoundly.)* Everyone.

(The song grows more distant.)

PONCIA: Quiet! Quiet!

REAPERS: Open your doors and your windows
    you women that live in this town
    the reaper asks for roses
    to decorate his crown.

(Martirio sings with it, nostalgically. Adela with passion finishes it. The song gets further away.)

PONCIA: They're turning the corner.

ADELA: Let's watch from the window in my room.

PONCIA: Be careful not to open the shutters too wide: they like to give them a push to see who's looking.

(The three leave. Martirio is left sitting on the low chair with her head between her hands.)

AMELIA: *(Drawing near her.)* What's wrong with you?

MARTIRIO: The heat is making me sick.

AMELIA: Is that all?

MARTIRIO: I wish November would come, the rainy days, the frost, anything but this endless summer.

AMELIA: The summer will pass and it will come again.

MARTIRIO: Well of course. *(Pause.)* What time did you go to sleep last night?

AMELIA: I don't know. I sleep like a log. Why?

MARTIRIO: Nothing. But I thought I heard people in the corral.

AMELIA: Oh?

MARTIRIO: Very late.

AMELIA: And you weren't scared?

MARTIRIO: No. I've heard it other nights.

AMELIA: We should be careful. Couldn't it have been the farm hands?

MARTIRIO: The farm hands come at six.

AMELIA: Maybe a young, unbroken mule.

MARTIRIO: *(Between her teeth.)* Yes, that's it, a young, unbroken, mule.

AMELIA: We should all keep watch.

MARTIRIO: No, no don't say anything. Maybe I imagined it.

AMELIA: Maybe. *(Pause. Amelia starts to go.)*

MARTIRIO: Amelia!

AMELIA: *(At the door.)* What?
　　　(Pause.)

MARTIRIO: Nothing.
　　　(Pause.)

AMELIA: Why did you call me?
　　　(Pause.)

MARTIRIO: It just came out. I wasn't thinking.
　　　(Pause.)

AMELIA: Go and lie down for a while.

ANGUSTIAS: *(Bursts in furiously, in a manner that makes a great contrast with previous quiet scene.)* Where is the picture of Pepe I had under my pillow? Which one of you took it?

MARTIRIO: No one.

AMELIA: It's not like he's Saint Bartholomew.
　　　(Poncia, Magdalena and Adela enter.)

ANGUSTIAS: Where is the picture?

ADELA: What picture?

ANGUSTIAS: The picture of Pepe, one of you has hidden it from me.

MAGDALENA: You have the audacity to say that?

ANGUSTIAS: It was in my room and it's not there now!

MARTIRIO: Couldn't it have slipped out into the corral in the middle of the night? Pepe likes to walk in the moonlight.

ANGUSTIAS: Don't play games with me! When he comes I'll tell him!

PONCIA: *(Looking at Adela.)* No, don't do that. It'll turn up.

ANGUSTIAS: I would like to know which one of you has it?

ADELA: *(Looking at Martirio.)* Well somebody—everybody! does, but not me.

MARTIRIO: *(With meaning.)* Naturally, never you.

BERNARDA: *(Entering, with her cane.)* What is this commotion in my house? In the silence of the heat of the day? The neighbors will have their ears glued to the walls.

ANGUSTIAS: They've taken the picture of my fiancé.

BERNARDA: Who? Who?

ANGUSTIAS: Them!

BERNARDA: Which of you? *(Silence.)* Answer me! *(Silence. To Poncia.)* Search their rooms: look in the beds. *(To Daughters.)* This comes from giving you too long a leash. But I'll haunt your dreams. *(To Angustias.)* Are you sure?

ANGUSTIAS: Yes.

BERNARDA: You looked carefully?

ANGUSTIAS: Yes, mother.

(They all stand around in embarrassed silence.)

BERNARDA: At the end of my life you force me to drink the most bitter poison a mother can bear. *(To Poncia.)* You didn't find it?

(Poncia enters.)

PONCIA: Here it is.

BERNARDA: Where was it?

PONCIA: It...was...

BERNARDA: Don't be afraid to say it.

PONCIA: *(In a surprised manner.)* ...In between the sheets of Martirio's bed.

BERNARDA: *(To Martirio.)* Is this true?

MARTIRIO: It's true.

(Advancing on her, beating her with her cane.)

BERNARDA: I'd like to squash you like an insect under my foot! You scorpion, you snake-in-the grass!

MARTIRIO: *(Furious, using the formal.)* Don't you hit me, Mother!

BERNARDA: I'll hit you all I want!

MARTIRIO: If I let you. You hear me? Get away from me!

PONCIA: Don't be disrespectful to your mother.

ANGUSTIAS: *(Holding Bernarda.)* Leave her alone. Please.

BERNARDA: Not even a tear.

MARTIRIO: I'm not going to cry to please you!

BERNARDA: Why did you take the picture?

MARTIRIO: Can't I play a joke on my own sister? Why else would I want it?

ADELA: *(Leaping forward, full of jealousy.)* It wasn't a joke, you never liked playing games. It was something else, bursting to come out. Say it!

MARTIRIO: You be quiet, and don't you make me speak, because if I do, the walls will fold in on each other for shame!

ADELA: A wicked tongue never stops inventing lies.

BERNARDA: Adela!

MAGDALENA: You're both mad.

AMELIA: And you torture us with your shameful thoughts.

MARTIRIO: Some people do shameful things.

ADELA: Until they strip naked and the river sweeps them away.

BERNARDA: You are *perverse!*

ANGUSTIAS: It's not my fault Pepe el Romano chose me.

ADELA: For your money.

ANGUSTIAS: Mother!

MARTIRIO: For your fields and your orchards.

BERNARDA: Silence!

MAGDALENA: It's the truth.

BERNARDA: Silence, I said! I could see the storm brewing, but I didn't think it would break so soon. Oh, you've laid a heavy stone of hatred on my heart. But I'm not old yet, and I'll chain up the five of you in this house my father built, so not even the weeds in the yard will know of my anguish. Get out! All of you!

(They go out. Bernarda sits down desolately. La Poncia is standing close to the wall. Bernarda recovers herself, and beats on the floor.)

BERNARDA: Use a firm hand Bernarda, remember, you have obligations.

PONCIA: May I speak?

BERNARDA: Speak. I'm sorry you heard that. It's never wise to have an outsider in a family.

PONCIA: What I've seen, I've seen.

BERNARDA: Angustias must get married right away.

PONCIA: Of course. We'll have to get her away from here.

BERNARDA: Not her. Him!

PONCIA: Of course. He's the one to get away from here—good thinking.

BERNARDA: I don't think. There are things one cannot and should not think. I give orders.

PONCIA: Do you think he'll want to go away?

BERNARDA: *(Rising.)* What do you mean?

PONCIA: He will of course be marrying Angustias.

BERNARDA: Speak up! I know you well enough to know when you've got your knife out for me.

PONCIA: I never knew a warning could be called murder.

BERNARDA: You have a warning for me?

PONCIA: Bernarda, I'm not making accusations, I'm just saying open your eyes, and you'll see.

BERNARDA: See what?

PONCIA: You've always been smart. You can spot the worst in other people from a hundred miles away: Sometimes I think you can read their thoughts. But one's children are one's children. Now you're being blind.

BERNARDA: Are you talking about Martirio...

PONCIA: Alright, Martirio. *(With curiosity.)* I wonder why she took that picture.

BERNARDA: *(Shielding her daughter.)* She says it was a joke. What else could it be?

PONCIA: *(With energy.)* Do you really believe that?

BERNARDA: Yes!

PONCIA: Alright, we are talking about your own. But what if we were talking about the neighbors from across the way?

BERNARDA: Now you're starting to sharpen the knife.

PONCIA: Bernarda, something very wrong is going on here. I don't want to put the blame on you, but you've never given your daughters any freedom. Martirio is sick for love, I don't care what you say. Why didn't you let her marry Enrique Humanes? Why, on the day he was to come to her window, why did you send him word not to come?

BERNARDA: And I'd do it a thousand times over! My blood will not mix with the blood of the Humanes as long as I live! His father was a farm hand!

PONCIA: Look what's come of putting on airs.

BERNARDA: I put them on because I can afford to, and you cannot, because you know what you come from.

PONCIA: *(With hatred.)* Don't remind me. I'm an old woman. I've always been grateful for your protection.

BERNARDA: You don't show it.

PONCIA: *(With hate masked by sweetness.)* Martirio will forget about this.

BERNARDA: And if she doesn't forget, so much the worse for her. I don't think something 'very wrong' is going on here. That's what you'd like to believe. And if one day something should happen, you can be sure it won't get beyond these walls.

PONCIA: I wouldn't be too sure of that. There are other people in this village who can read thoughts at a distance.

BERNARDA: How you would love to see me and my daughters on our way to the whorehouse!

PONCIA: No one knows their own end.

BERNARDA: I know mine! And my daughters! The whorehouse was for a certain woman now dead.

PONCIA: *(Furious.)* Bernarda, respect the memory of my mother.

BERNARDA: Then stop plaguing me with your wicked thoughts!
(Pause.)

PONCIA: Better if I stay out of everything.

BERNARDA: That's right. Work. Keep your mouth shut. The duty of all who work for hire.

PONCIA: I can't do that. Don't you think it would be better if Pepe were married to Martirio or...yes!, or to Adela?

BERNARDA: No, I don't think.

PONCIA: *(With meaning.)* Adela. Now there's the true bride for el Romano.

BERNARDA: Things are never the way we'd like them to be.

PONCIA: No, but it's hard work turning them from their true course. For Pepe to be with Angustias seems wrong to me—and to other people as well. And even to the wind. Who can tell if things will turn out as they should?

BERNARDA: Here you go again...! Sneaking up on me. My daughters respect me, and they have never gone against my will.

PONCIA: That's right! But the minute they break free, they'll climb to the rooftops.

BERNARDA: Then I'll throw stones at them to bring them down.

PONCIA: You were always the bravest.

BERNARDA: I've always enjoyed a good fight.

PONCIA: Isn't it strange? You should see the fever Angustias is in over her lover. At her age! And it seems he's smitten, too. Yesterday, my oldest son told me that when he passed by with the oxen at four thirty in the morning, they were still there talking at the window.

BERNARDA: At four thirty?

ANGUSTIAS: *(Entering.)* That's a lie!

PONCIA: That's what he told me.

BERNARDA: *(To Angustias.)* Talk.

ANGUSTIAS: For over a week Pepe has been leaving at one o'clock. May God strike me dead if I'm lying.

MARTIRIO: *(Entering.)* I heard him leave at four too.

BERNARDA: Did you see him with your own eyes?

MARTIRIO: I didn't want to be seen. Don't you go to the side window to talk now?

ANGUSTIAS: We talk at my bedroom window.

(Adela appears at the door.)

MARTIRIO: Then…

BERNARDA: What is going on in this house?

PONCIA: Careful or you'll find out. All I know is that Pepe was at one of your windows—at half past four in the morning.

BERNARDA: Are you sure?

PONCIA: You can't be sure of anything in this life.

ADELA: Mother, don't listen to her, she wants to ruin us all.

BERNARDA: I know how to find out. If people in this town want to spread lies about me, they'll find they've run into a stone wall. No one is to talk about this! or waves of filth could drown us all.

MARTIRIO: I don't like to lie.

PONCIA: Then something is going to happen.

BERNARDA: Nothing is going to happen. I was born to keep my eyes open and I won't shut them now until the day I die.

ANGUSTIAS: I have the right to know.

BERNARDA: You have the right to nothing except to do what I tell you. No one tells me what I can or can not do. *(To Poncia.)* You put your own house in order. Nothing happens here without my knowing about it.

MAID: *(Entering.)* There's a big crowd at the top of the street and all the neighbors are at their doors.

BERNARDA: *(To Poncia.)* You, run and see what's going on.

(The girls are about to run out.)

BERNARDA: Where do you think you're going? You women, staring at doorways, breaking your mourning. Go to your rooms, all of you!

(They go out. Bernarda leaves. Distant shouts are heard. Martirio and Adela enter and listen, not daring to step further than the front door.)

MARTIRIO: You're lucky I didn't open my mouth.

ADELA: I could have said something, too.

MARTIRIO: What could you have said? You won't go on like this much longer.

ADELA: I'll have it all.

MARTIRIO: I'll tear you out of his arms.

ADELA: Martirio, leave me alone.

MARTIRIO: None of us will have him!

ADELA: He wants to live with me.

MARTIRIO: I saw how he was holding you.

ADELA: I didn't want this. It's as if I'm being dragged by a rope.

MARTIRIO: I'll see you dead first.

(Magdalena and Angustias look in. The tumult is increasing. Poncia enters with Bernarda from another door.)

PONCIA: Bernarda!

BERNARDA: What is going on?

PONCIA: It's Librada's daughter, the unmarried one, had a baby, and nobody knows whose it is.

ADELA: A baby?

PONCIA: And to hide her shame, she killed it and buried it under the rocks, but some dogs dug it up and left it at her door. Now they want to kill her. They're dragging her through the streets.

BERNARDA: Good, let them come, let them bring olive switches and pick handles. Let them come and kill her.

ADELA: No! No! Not kill her!

MARTIRIO: Yes,—let us go out there too!

BERNARDA: Any woman who tramples on her decency must pay for it.

(Outside a woman's shriek and a great clamor is heard.)

ADELA: Let her escape! Don't go out there!

MARTIRIO: *(Looking at Adela.)* Let her pay what she owes!

BERNARDA: *(At the archway.)* Finish her off before the police get here. Fiery coals in the place where she sinned.

ADELA: *(Holding her belly.)* No! No!

BERNARDA: Kill her! Kill her!

BERNARDA & MARTIRIO: Kill her! Kill her! Kill her!

(Curtain.)

End of Act II

ACT III

It is night. The doorways, illuminated by the lights inside the rooms, give a glow to the stage. At the center there is a table with a shaded oil lamp around which Bernarda and her daughters are eating. La Poncia serves them. Prudencia sits apart. When the curtain rises, there is a great silence interrupted only by the noise of plates and silverware.

PRUDENCIA: *(She rises.)* I'm going, Bernarda. It's been a long visit.

BERNARDA: Wait, Prudencia. We never see each other.

PRUDENCIA: Have they sounded the last bell for the rosary?

PONCIA: Not yet.

(Prudencia sits down again.)

BERNARDA: And your husband, how is he?

PRUDENCIA: The same.

BERNARDA: We never see him either.

PRUDENCIA: You know how he is. Ever since he fought his brothers over the inheritance he won't use the front door. He puts up a ladder and climbs over the back wall.

BERNARDA: A real man! And your daughter?

PRUDENCIA: He has never forgiven her.

BERNARDA: He's right.

PRUDENCIA: I don't know about that.

BERNARDA: A daughter who disobeys stops being a daughter and becomes an enemy.

PRUDENCIA: I let water run.

(A heavy blow is heard against the walls.)

PRUDENCIA: What was that?

BERNARDA: The stallion. He's tied in his stall and he's kicking against the wall. *(Shouting.)* Tether him and take him out in the yard! *(In a lower voice.)* He must be too hot.

PRUDENCIA: Are you going to put him to the new mares?

BERNARDA: At daylight.

PRUDENCIA: You've known how to increase your stock.

BERNARDA: Through a lot of money and hard work.

PONCIA: *(Interrupting.)* She has the best herd in this part of the country. It's too bad the prices are down.

BERNARDA: Do you want some cheese, or some honey?

PRUDENCIA: I have no appetite.

(The blow is heard again.)

PONCIA: Oh for God's sake!

PRUDENCIA: I can feel it right through my chest.

BERNARDA: *(Rising, furiously.)* Do I have to say everything twice? Let him out to roll in the straw!

(Pause. Then, as though speaking to the stableman.)

BERNARDA: Tether the mares in the corral, but let him run free, or he'll kick the walls down. *(She returns to the table and sits again.)* Ay! What a life!

PRUDENCIA: You have to fight like a man.

BERNARDA: That's it.

(Adela gets up from the table.)

BERNARDA: Where are you going?

ADELA: For a drink of water.

BERNARDA: *(Raising her voice.)* Bring a pitcher of fresh water. *(To Adela.)* You can sit down.

(Adela sits down.)

PRUDENCIA: And Angustias, when will she be married?

BERNARDA: They come to ask for her in three days.

PRUDENCIA: You must be happy.

BERNARDA: *(Pause.)* Angustias.

ANGUSTIAS: Of course.

AMELIA: *(To Magdalena.)* You spilled the salt!

MAGDALENA: You can't have worse luck than you're already having.

AMELIA: It's always a bad sign.

BERNARDA: That's enough.

PRUDENCIA: *(To Angustias.)* Has he given you the ring yet?

ANGUSTIAS: See? *(She holds it out.)*

PRUDENCIA: It's beautiful. Three pearls. In my day, pearls meant tears.

ANGUSTIAS: Well, things have changed.

ADELA: Things don't change their meaning. Engagement rings should be diamonds.

PRUDENCIA: The most appropriate.

BERNARDA: With or without pearls, life is what you make it.

MARTIRIO: Or what God makes for you.

PRUDENCIA: I've been told your furniture is beautiful.

BERNARDA: It ought to be. I spent sixteen thousand *reales*.

PRUDENCIA: What's important is everything is for the best.

ADELA: And you never know.

BERNARDA: There's no reason why it shouldn't be.

(Bells are heard very distantly.)

PRUDENCIA: The last bell. *(To Angustias.)* I'll come back soon and you can show me the dress.

ANGUSTIAS: Whenever you like.

PRUDENCIA: Good night. God be with you.

BERNARDA: Goodbye, Prudencia.

ALL FIVE DAUGHTERS: *(At the same time.)* God be with you.

(Pause. Prudencia goes out.)

BERNARDA: Well, we've eaten. That's done.

(They rise.)

ADELA: I'm going to walk to the front gate and stretch my legs.

(Magdalena sits down in a low chair and leans against the wall.)

AMELIA: I'll go with you.

MARTIRIO: Me too.

ADELA: *(With contained hate.)* I won't get lost.

AMELIA: You should have company at night.

(They go out. Bernarda sits down. Angustias is clearing the table.)

BERNARDA: I told you once already! I want you to speak with your sister Martirio. What happened with the picture was a joke and you should forget about it.

ANGUSTIAS: You know she hates me.

BERNARDA: Each of us knows what we think inside. I don't pry into people's hearts, but I do insist you keep up appearances and we have peace in the family. Understood?

ANGUSTIAS: Yes.

BERNARDA: Then that's settled.

MAGDALENA: *(She is almost asleep.)* Anyway, you're going to be leaving soon...

(She falls asleep.)

ANGUSTIAS: Not soon enough for me.

BERNARDA: What time did you finish talking last night?

ANGUSTIAS: At half past twelve.

BERNARDA: What does Pepe talk about?

ANGUSTIAS: He's distracted. He always talks to me as if he was thinking of something else. When I ask him what's wrong, he says "We men have our worries."

BERNARDA: Then don't ask him. Especially once you are married. Speak if he speaks, look at him when he looks at you. That way you'll get along.

ANGUSTIAS: Mother, I think he's hiding a lot of things from me.

BERNARDA: Don't try and find out what they are. Don't ask him, and above all never let him see you cry.

ANGUSTIAS: I should be happy, and I'm not.

BERNARDA: It's all the same.

ANGUSTIAS: Some nights I stare at him through the window bars, and he seems to fade away, like he's being covered by a cloud of dust kicked up by the sheep.

BERNARDA: It's because you're not strong.

ANGUSTIAS: I hope it's that.

BERNARDA: Is he coming tonight?

ANGUSTIAS: No. He went to the city with his mother.

BERNARDA: Then we'll get to bed early. Magdalena?

ANGUSTIAS: She's asleep.

(Adela, Martirio, and Amelia enter.)

AMELIA: It's such a dark night!

ADELA: You can't see two steps in front of you.

MARTIRIO: A good night for thieves, or anybody who needs to hide.

ADELA: The stallion was in the middle of the corral. White! Looking twice as big as usual! He filled up the darkness.

AMELIA: It looked like a ghost.

ADELA: There are stars in the sky as big as fists.

MARTIRIO: (About Adela.) This one was staring at them until she almost broke her neck.

ADELA: Don't you like them?

MARTIRIO: I don't care what goes on above the rooftops. I have enough to handle with what goes on down here.

ADELA: Well, that's the way it is for you.

BERNARDA: It's the same for you as it is for her.

ANGUSTIAS: Good night.

ADELA: Are you going to bed now?

ANGUSTIAS: Yes. Pepe isn't coming tonight. (Angustias exits.)

ADELA: Mother, why do people cross themselves every time there's a shooting star or a flash of lightning?

BERNARDA: Oh, the old people know lots of things we've forgotten.

AMELIA: I close my eyes so I won't see them.

ADELA: Not me. I like to see what's been quiet for years and years suddenly shoot fire.

MARTIRIO: All that has nothing to do with us.

BERNARDA: Best not to think about them.

ADELA: Oh what a beautiful night! I'd like to stay up and feel the cool breeze from the fields.

BERNARDA: But we have to go to bed. Magdalena!

AMELIA: She's asleep.

BERNARDA: Magdalena!

MAGDALENA: Leave me alone.

BERNARDA: Go to bed!

MAGDALENA: *(Rising, in a bad humor.)* You don't give anyone a moment's peace. *(She goes off grumbling.)*

AMELIA: Good night. *(She goes out.)*

BERNARDA: You two off to bed too.

MARTIRIO: Why isn't Angustias's fiancé coming tonight?

BERNARDA: He went on a trip.

MARTIRIO: *(Looking at Adela.)* Ah!

ADELA: Goodnight.

(She goes out. Martirio drinks some water and goes out slowly, looking at the door to the yard. La Poncia enters.)

PONCIA: Are you still here?

BERNARDA: I'm enjoying the quiet and unable to see the "something very wrong" that is "going on" here, according to you.

PONCIA: Bernarda, let's not go any further with this.

BERNARDA: In this house there's one way of doing things. My watchfulness takes care of everything.

PONCIA: Nothing is going on outwardly. That's true. But your daughters live as if they were locked up in a cupboard. Neither you nor anyone else can see into their hearts.

BERNARDA: My daughters' hearts beat calmly enough.

PONCIA: That's your business. You're their mother. I have enough to do looking after your house.

BERNARDA: Yes. Now you've turned quiet.

PONCIA: I keep my place—that's all.

BERNARDA: Your problem is you have nothing to say. If there were weeds growing in this house, you'd make sure all the sheep in the neighborhood came here to graze.

PONCIA: I hide more than you think.

BERNARDA: Do your sons still see Pepe here at four in the morning? Do they still spread the same malicious gossip about this house?

PONCIA: They say nothing.

BERNARDA: Because there's nothing they can say. No meat to sink their teeth into, thanks to my vigilance.

PONCIA: Bernarda, I don't want to talk about this because I'm afraid of what you'll do. But don't be too sure.

BERNARDA: Oh, but I am. Very sure.

PONCIA: Lightening could strike. A rush of blood could suddenly stop your heart.

BERNARDA: Nothing will happen here. I'm on guard now against all your suspicions.

PONCIA: All the better for you.

BERNARDA: *(She rises.)* Exactly.

(The maid enters.)

MAID: I've just finished the dishes. Is there anything else, Bernarda?

BERNARDA: Nothing. I'm going to get some rest.

PONCIA: What time do you want me to wake you?

BERNARDA: Don't. I intend to sleep soundly tonight. *(She goes out.)*

PONCIA: When you are powerless against the sea, it's better to turn your back on it so you don't see it.

MAID: She's so proud, she puts a blindfold on herself.

PONCIA: Well, there's nothing I can do. I tried to put a stop to this, but now—It frightens me too much. Feel the silence? In every room, a storm is brewing, and the day it breaks it'll sweep us all away. I said what I had to say.

MAID: Bernarda thinks nothing can stand against her. She doesn't know the power of a man among women alone.

PONCIA: It's not all Pepe el Romano's fault. It's true last year he chased after Adela and she was crazy about him, but Adela should have kept her place and not led him on. A man is a man.

MAID: Some say he's talked to Adela many nights.

PONCIA: It's true. *(Whispers.)* And that's not all.

MAID: Bernarda's rushing the wedding: maybe nothing will happen.

PONCIA: No, things have gone too far already. Adela's made up her mind, whatever happens, and the others constantly keep watch.

MAID: Martirio, too?

PONCIA: That one's the worst. She's a pool of poison. She knows she can't get el Romano herself, and she'd drown the whole world if it was in her power.

MAID: They're bad!

PONCIA: They're women without men, that's all. In matters like these you even forget your own blood. Sssshh! *(She listens.)*

MAID: What is it?

PONCIA: The dogs are barking.

MAID: Someone must have passed by the front door.

(Adela enters wearing a white petticoat and a corselet.)

PONCIA: Didn't you go to bed?

ADELA: I'm getting a drink of water. *(She drinks from a glass on the table.)*

PONCIA: I thought you were asleep.

ADELA: I got thirsty. What about you, don't you ever rest?

MAID: Soon now.

(Adela goes out.)

PONCIA: Let's go.

MAID: We've earned some sleep. Bernarda doesn't let me rest the whole day.

PONCIA: Take the lamp.

MAID: The dogs are going mad.

PONCIA: They're not going to let us sleep.

(They go out. The stage is left almost dark. Maria Josefa enters with a lamb in her arms.)

MARIA JOSEFA: *(Singing.)* Little lamb, child of mine
Let's go to the shore of the sea
The little ant is at his door
I'll give you my breast and bread
Bernarda
Face of a leopard
Magdalena of a hyena
Little lamb
Baa! Baa! Baa!
We'll go to the palms at Bethlehem's gate
You and I won't want to sleep
A door will open on its own
On the beach you and I
will hide in a hut of coral reef.
Bernarda
Face of a leopard
Magdalena
of a hyena
Little lamb, baaa, baaa
We'll go to the palms at Bethlehem's gate.

(Adela enters and runs to the corral door as Maria Josefa pounds on the front door. Martirio enters.)

MARTIRIO: Grandmother, where are you going?

MARIA JOSEFA: Have you come to open the door for me? Who are you?

MARTIRIO: How did you get out here?

MARIA JOSEFA: I escaped. Which one are you?

MARTIRIO: Go back to bed.

MARIA JOSEFA: Oh, now I see you. Martirio, face of a martyr. And when are you going to have a baby? I've had this one.

MARTIRIO: Where did you get that lamb?

MARIA JOSEFA: I know it's a lamb. But why can't a lamb be a baby? It's better to have a lamb than to have nothing. Bernarda, face of a leopard. Magdalena, of a hyena.

MARTIRIO: Don't shout.

MARIA JOSEFA: It's true. Everything is dark. Because my hair is white you think I can't have babies. Babies and babies and babies. This baby will have white hair, and will have another baby and all with white hair, like snow. We'll be like the waves, one after another. And then we'll sit down and we'll all have white heads and we'll be the foam of the sea. Why isn't there any foam here? Nothing but mourning shawls.

MARTIRIO: Shh, Shh.

MARIA JOSEFA: When my neighbor had a baby, I took her some chocolate, and later, she brought me some—always and always and always. You'll have white hair, but your neighbors won't come. I have to go now, but I'm afraid the dogs may bite me. Will you come with me out to the fields? I don't like the fields. I like houses, but open houses with the women stretched out on their beds with their little children, and the men outside sitting on their chairs. Pepe el Romano is a giant! Every one of you loves him. But he'll devour you because you're all just grains of wheat. No, not grains of wheat. Frogs without tongues.

MARTIRIO: Go to bed. *(She pushes her.)*

MARIA JOSEFA: Yes. But later you'll open the door for me. Won't you?

MARTIRIO: Of course.

MARIA JOSEFA: *(Weeping. Sings her lullaby.)* Ah, little lamb, child of mine
Let's go to the shore of the sea
The little ant will be at his door
I'll give you my breast and bread.
(She goes. Martirio closes the door on Maria Josepha, locks it and goes to the yard door. There she hesitates, but goes two steps further.)

MARTIRIO: *(Low voice.)* Adela. *(Pause. Louder.)* Adela!

(Adela enters. Her hair is disarranged.)

ADELA: Why are you looking for me?

MARTIRIO: Stay away from that man!

ADELA: Who are you to tell me?

MARTIRIO: That's no place for a decent woman.

ADELA: How you would love to take my place!

MARTIRIO: *(Louder.)* This can't continue.

ADELA: This is only the beginning. I have the strength to do it, and the spirit, and the looks, which you don't have. I saw death under this roof and I went out to look for what is mine, for what belongs to me.

MARTIRIO: That man without a soul, came here for another woman. You put yourself between them.

ADELA: He came for the money, but his eyes were always on me.

MARTIRIO: I won't let you steal him. He will marry Angustias.

ADELA: You know he doesn't love her.

MARTIRIO: I know that.

ADELA: You know because you've seen—he loves me!

MARTIRIO: *(Despairing.)* Yes!

ADELA: *(Coming closer to her.)* He loves me! He loves me!

MARTIRIO: Stick me with a knife if you want, just don't say that again!

ADELA: That's why you're trying to stop me from going away with him. It makes no difference to you if he's putting his arms around someone he doesn't love: I don't care either. He could spend a hundred years with Angustias, but if he's holding me, caressing me, you can't stand it because you're in love with him too. You love him!

MARTIRIO: Yes! Let me say it without shame! Yes! My heart is bursting with envy. I love him!

ADELA: *(Impulsively, hugging her.)* Martirio, Martirio, it's not my fault.

MARTIRIO: Don't touch me! My blood isn't yours anymore. No matter how much I want to see you as a sister, I can only see you as another woman. *(She pushes her away.)*

ADELA: Then there's no way out. Whoever has to drown will drown. Pepe el Romano is mine. He will carry me away to the reeds by the sea.

MARTIRIO: He will not.

ADELA: I can't stand the horror of being under this roof any more, not after tasting his mouth. I will be what he wants me to be. All the village against me, burning me with their pointing fingers, persecuted by those who call themselves decent people, and I will put on, in front of them all, the crown of thorns that belongs to the mistresses of married men.

MARTIRIO: Be quiet!

ADELA: Yes, we'll let him marry Angustias, it's not important to me, but I'll move to a little house by myself, where he'll come and see me whenever he wants, whenever he desires me.

MARTIRIO: Not if there's a drop of blood in my body.

ADELA: You can't stop me. You're weak. I could bring a wild stallion to its knees with the strength of my little finger.

MARTIRIO: Don't you raise your voice at me, I can't stand it. My heart is full of a force so vicious, I can't stop it from drowning me.

ADELA: They teach us to love our sisters. God must have abandoned me in this darkness, because I see you now as if I'd never seen you anywhere before.

(A whistle is heard at the front door and Adela runs toward the door, but Martirio gets in front of her.)

MARTIRIO: Where are you going?

ADELA: Move away from that door!

MARTIRIO: Get by me if you can!

ADELA: Get away!

(They struggle.)

MARTIRIO: *(Shouts.)* Mother! Mother!

ADELA: Let me go!

(Bernarda enters. She wears petticoats and a black shawl.)

BERNARDA: Stop this! Oh, how I wish I could make lightening strike.

MARTIRIO: *(Pointing to Adela.)* She was with him! Look at her, she's covered with straw!

BERNARDA: *(Going furiously toward Adela.)* The bed of a whore.

ADELA: *(Facing her.)* Here ends my imprisonment! *(She snatches her mother's cane and breaks it in two.)* That's what I do with the warden's rod. Do not take another step! No one gives me orders here except Pepe!

MAGDALENA: *(Entering.)* Adela!

(Poncia and Angustias enter.)

ADELA: I belong to him! *(To Angustias.)* Accept it. He will be master of this house. Go out in the yard and tell him. He's out there now, panting like a lion.

ANGUSTIAS: My God!

BERNARDA: The gun, where is the gun!

(Bernarda rushes out. Martirio exits behind her. Amelia enters and looks on frightened, leaning her head against the wall. Adela tries to run out.)

ANGUSTIAS: *(Holding her.)* You're not leaving here, to triumph with your body! You thief! You shame our house!

MAGDALENA: Let her go where we never have to see her again!

(A shot is heard.)

BERNARDA: *(Entering.)* Find him now, if you dare.

MARTIRIO: *(Entering.)* That's the end of it.

ADELA: Pe-pe! My God! Pepe! *(She runs out.)*

PONCIA: Did you kill him?

MARTIRIO: No. He galloped away on his horse.

BERNARDA: It was my fault. A woman can't aim.

MAGDALENA: Then why did you say…?

MARTIRIO: For her! I'd like to pour a river of blood over her.

PONCIA: Damn you!

MAGDALENA: You devil!

BERNARDA: It's better this way.

(A thud is heard.)

BERNARDA: Adela? Adela?

PONCIA: *(At the door.)* Open the door.

BERNARDA: Open the door! Don't think the walls will hide your shame.

MAID: *(Entering.)* All the neighbors are up!

BERNARDA: *(In a low voice, but like a roar.)* Open the door, or I'll break it down!

(Pause. Everything is silent.)

BERNARDA: *(She walks away from the door.)* Adela!

(La Poncia throws herself against the door. It opens and she goes in. As she enters, she screams and backs out.)

BERNARDA: What is it?

PONCIA: *(Puts her hands to her throat.)* May we never die like that!

(The sisters fall back. The maid crosses herself. Bernarda screams and goes forward.)

BERNARDA: Aaaarrrgghhh!

PONCIA: Don't go in!

BERNARDA: No…Pepe—you run, alive, in the darkness under the poplar trees, but, one day, you'll fall. Cut her down! Carry her to her room and dress her in white. No one is to say anything. Send word to toll the bells twice at dawn.

MARTIRIO: She's a thousand times happier to have what she's had.

BERNARDA: And I want no tears. Death must be looked at face to face. Tears are for when you are alone! We shall all of us drown in a sea of mourning. The youngest daughter of Bernarda Alba died a virgin. Did you hear me? Silence, silence I said. Silence.

THE END

ESCAPE FROM PARADISE

Regina Taylor

He that will enter into Paradise must come with the right key.
THOMAS FULLER

It will fill any space you give it...So broad—
it takes in all things true; so narrow—it can hold but you.
JOHN R. MORELAND

These two
Imparadised in one another's arms,
The happier Eden, shall enjoy their fill
of bliss on bliss...
JOHN MILTON

Paradise hath room for you and me and all.
CHRISTINA G. ROSSETTI

Who has not found the heaven below will fail of it above.
EMILY DICKINSON

Adam, whiles he spake not, had Paradise at will.
WILLIAM LANGLAND

Thou Paradise of exiles, Italy!
PERCY BYSSHE SHELLEY

THE AUTHOR

Regina Taylor is an associate artist at the Goodman Theater and the Alliance Theater. She is also a writer of children's books, plays, poems, and short stories. As an actress she has appeared on Broadway as Juliet in *Romeo and Juliet,* won a Dramalogue award as Ariel in *The Tempest,* and was featured in the films *Lean on Me, Clockers,* and television's *Children of the Dust, Law and Order,* and *The Howard Beach Story.* For her role as Lilly Harper in *I'll Fly Away,* Ms. Taylor won an NAACP Image Award, Viewers for Quality TV Award, was nominated for an Emmy and won the Golden Globe Award for best leading dramatic actress. Her plays include *OO-BLA-DEE, Watermelon Rinds, Mudtracks, Ghost Story, Sty Farm, Between the Lines, Inside the Belly of the Beast,* and her one-woman show *Escape from Paradise.* In addition to numerous workshops and readings, her plays have been produced at the Goodman Theater, the Actors Theater of Louisville Humana Festival, the Circle Rep, the Alliance Theater, and the Ensemble Studio Theatre One-Act Festival. *OO-BLA-DEE* will have a workshop this summer with the prestigeous Sundance Theatre Lab and is scheduled for production with the Goodman Theatre in the spring. Ms. Taylor has received commissions from the Goodman Theater, the Actors Theatre of Louisville Humana Festival, and the Alliance Theater.

ARIADNE AND
THE ESCAPE FROM PARADISE

Paradise is a walled garden...

Ariadne, princess daughter of powerful King Minos, had never been outside the carefully tended gardens of her father's Palace at Knossos, and the only man she had ever seen besides her father was the aging palace architect, Daedalus.

But upon seeing Theseus, the golden-haired and god-like champion of Athens, Ariadne fell instantly in love with him.

Paradise is going into the labyrinth—
searching for the minotaur—and finding your way back...

Theseus had been sent to Knossos as part of a long-standing war tribute to King Minos. He had been sentenced to enter the Labyrinth, the dreaded wooden maze that meant certain death, either by starvation or at the claws of the Minotaur—the half-man-half-bull-all-monster who roamed its darkened corridors.

Determined to see her first and only love survive the Labyrinth, Ariadne smuggled a magic sword to Theseus and also handed him a spool of thread so he could retrace his steps through the maze.

With sword, thread, and Ariadne's love, Theseus charged into the Labyrinth, slew the Minotaur, and followed the thread to the safety and warmth of his betrothed. Further following her instructions to escape, Theseus gashed the keels of Minos' navy fleet so the King could not follow their flight, and together, they sailed for Athens.

Paradise is a one night stand...

Ariadne was sickened by the waves of the sea and by the guilt of betraying her father and her homeland, so Theseus grounded the ships on the island of Naxos and urged Ariadne to rest. The gentle rhythm of the sea put her mind at ease, and Ariadne soon fell asleep on the warm beach sand. When she awakened, Theseus and the ships were gone. Whether he had abandoned her, had forgotten her, or had been swept out to sea without her, Ariadne stood on the shores alone.

She waded into the sea, searching the horizon for a sign of her lover Theseus and began to weep. Whe cursed Theseus and prayed that equal grief and betrayal fall upon him and his family. The young God Bacchus saw Ariadne in the water and was immediately enraptured by her beauty. He flew to her side, wrapped her in his powerful god arms, and swore eternal love to her.

Unlike Theseus, Bacchus followed through on his promises, living and loving Ariadne until she died. Grief-stricken, he removed the golden crown from her head—the crown he had given her on their wedding day—and hurled it into the northern night sky. There, the crown and the memory of Ariadne would shine for all eternity as the Corona Borealis.

Here I am taking pilgrimage #365—and
it always seems to be back when and over there.
I keep running—searching for that
elusive mercurial...something
Like trying to catch the minotaur by the tail. It keeps changing locations—
changing forms.
—from Escape from Paradise

ORIGINAL PRODUCTION

Escape from Paradise was originally produced at The Goodman Theatre, directed by Shirley Jo Finney, set design by Scott Cooper, projection design by Royd Climenhaga, lighting design by Robert Christen, sound design by Michael Bodeen, dramaturg Susan V. Booth, production stage manager Kimberly Osgood, and performed by Regina Taylor.

CHARACTERS

Sometimes you can read a person's life on their face—like a map. With Jenine the map is a jigsaw puzzle, each person she encounters on her journey is a part that makes her whole: Taxi Driver, Sister Sinclair, Superstar, Babs, Secretary, Terrinikka, Karen, Ronnie, Tour Guide, Rufus, Madear.

TIME AND PLACE

3:00 A.M. Between here and dream called Venice.

The set is a wall with a window—a table and chair sit center-stage. Stage left
is a microphone and a stool. An oversized easel (bolted to the floor) holds paper
that can be ripped away sits stage right. Through the windows we see images
projected of Jenine's imagination—landscapes—maps—parts of herself—her
eye-peers into the window—her hands—an arm, a leg—Parts of family pho-
tos—We see part of her mother, father, sister, brother, parts of Babs—the taxi
driver, and so on. The map of her life…Inside the drawer are red ink pens and
a journal which Jenine writes on. She uses blood red felt pens to write/draw on
the easel. On the walls are projected her blood red inkings. There is an exit
door. We hear music: "Long Journey Home" In the window, we see Jenine's
shadow running.

VOICE: Jenine's diary written on postcard #365 between here and a dream
called Venice was later revised as a book entitled—"How I Escaped
Paradise." Blackout.
(We hear overture of familiar sounds.)
VOICE: The mind of the traveler is like a sleepwalker—you are in different
times and places all at once.
(We see a shaft of light from a door—the door slams. Jenine has entered the
room.)
VOICE: How I Escaped Paradise—TAKE ONE.
(We hear wind.)
JENINE: How…today, instead of waking up and going to work, I bought a
ticket to Italy…by way of Rome to Florence to Venice…by way of the
Bronx—the Triborough Bridge…from California—the swaying watu-
sis…UTAH…Honking all the way to Grandpa's house. Today, instead
of waking up and going to work, I bought a ticket to Italy…Booked a
flight from L.A. to New York. I take a cab.
(We hear honking.)
(Int. Taxi. Eng. Rear view mirror with furry dice dangling.)
TAXI DRIVER: *(Radio plays salsa.)* Honk, Honk, Honk. Where to? Where to?
Which way do you want me to go? Say, you don't know the city? *(With*
a gleam.) Let's try going by way of the bridge, why don't we? How long
you been here for? Me—born in Kansas—you know Dorothy, clickin'
her fricken heels and such. Folks moved back to Kansas—couldn't take
it anymore. But, me and my husband—we don't give up on nothing—
you know. You know the difference between people born rich and people born poor? You know Dr. Seuss—you know the Dr. Seuss story—the
one about the sneetches. The uppity star-bellied sneetches looking down

on the sneetches without the stars on their bellies. So this guy—with this machine—he says, "This machine will put stars on your bellies"... (Gimme money gesture.) So they gave him their money. They go through the machine. They got stars on their bellies. They run over to the uppity star-bellied sneetches...they say, "Hey we're just like you now—there's no difference here—see." So don't you know these sneetches who had stars all along—they are pissed off. So that guy with the machine he tells them the machine can take off the stars— (Gimme money gesture.) They give him the money. They go through the machine...and they says, "Now we know who's who"—and so it goes back and forth. They pay the guy the money—they go through the machine—till everybody's broke and confused...I just ain't going through no fricken' machine. People live by machines. Tells you when to sleep...honey its not time to make love, its time to get up and go to work. Well I'm gonna fricken piss when I feel like pissin...make love whenever I want to...The only time that I care about is Times Square. No matter where you start from no matter where you goin—you always gonna have to pass through Times Square...*(Pats the heart in heartbeat rhythm.)* Kansas, Utah, Timbuktu, you gonna pass through Times Square *(Pats the heart.)* I got the open road. That's what make's me rich. Everything I pass, everything I see, everything I encounter, I own—without the labor. The Statue of Liberty to my first kiss. I got them in my trunk. Therefore, I have no envy and I have no fear. My folks don't understand—why they run back to Kansas for...Folks say, "Althea, Althea—why you gotta be zig zagging all around Manhattan? You want to make orphans of your three kids—you got *three kids.*" I got three kids—four, six and nine—two girls, the oldest is a boy—I read them Dr. Seuss. "You got three kids—got a husband"... Though they've never been fond of Marvin. They say, "Come home! Come home! Come home!—We got plenty of room." They live right off the golf course. My children could just as easily be hit by a golfball. Hit in the head and, God forbid, suffer massive brain damage from being hit by a fricken golf ball at grandma and grandpa's house as being shot down on the streets of fricken Manhattan—No thanks. What do you want me to do, click my fricken heels together or something? We'll take our chances here.

JENINE: Taxi driver takes me from Newark to La Guardia by way of the Bronx, by way of the Holland Tunnel, by way of Queens—the Staten Island Ferry—by way of Utah—to get me to the plane that would take me to Italy. Somehow, it makes sense—considering where I came from.

(We hear clock strike 3:00.)

JENINE: Three a.m.—I got on the plane with one carry-on bag. And I say—I'm leaving everything behind.

(Beat.)

(Int. Office.)

JENINE: Everything was going well. Work was good. I'd just negotiated a promotion with pay. I was a co-executive editor for a popular woman's magazine in California.

(We hear school bell.)

JENINE: I used to be a school teacher at a small elementary in Utah—that was before the divorce—after I bled all over the white carpet and wall in the house that Jack built. I ran to California. The beach and palm trees that looked like giant watusis swaying in the breeze—searching for a sign—listening for a calling. And I heard the voice of Sister Sinclair under the Santa Monica Pier.

(Ext. Under Santa Monica Pier.)

(Img. Water. Face half in shadow with closed eye.)

(We hear water.)

SISTER SINCLAIR: I have visions and my visions do come true. My visions—waking dreams of what will be. Carrying truth like the wind. Wind can lift you up and it can knock you down. I'm blind yet I can see. You got two eyes but you can't see me. Yes. Look around. Who do you see? You don't see nobody. You can't even see yourself. So busy searching, searching, searching for what? Some of you out there tonight know what I'm talking about. Me—I'm blind. I told the Lord—I'm tired. I said Lord—tired of looking around at all this forgetfulness and strife. I took my knitting needles and I saw the light thin and piercing opening up my eyes. Now I see it all. The good, the bad, the indifferent and all the shades in between. The hopeless, the helpless, the infirm come to me to know the way. See, we're all gonna die. That is the truth and we all want to know the pathway to paradise. Fifty dollars in one hand a little bit of faith in the other...You don't have fifty—then twenty five—ten—five cents. I know you got a nickel. A nickel and a cup of Cheerios. Come to Sister Sinclair. I'll set you straight. I'll lead you home to glory. I once was blind but now I see. Yes. My palm is open this evening. Will you take my hand and follow me.

JENINE: I gave Sister Sinclair a twenty dollar bill. She gave me a red spool of thread and whispered in my ear—

SISTER SINCLAIR: Paradise is going into the labyrinth—searching for the minotaur—and finding your way back.

JENINE: Twenty dollars bought me those words and a red spool of thread.

(Img. Red lines/words.)

(Beat.)

JENINE: I decided my calling was to become a writer. Threading together sentences, weaving words into walls where inside I could live in peace and solitude. *(Phone rings.)* The *reality* was earning a living. I was a freelancer for supermarket tabloids interviewing Hollywood personalities who had made it.

(Int. Penthouse.)

SUPERSTAR: *(To Jenine.)* Hold that thought—will you. *(To phone.)* Hello. Tell him to kiss my butt. You heard me—Kiss my butt. *(Snorts and stamps.)* Hello what? Yeah—tell him that for me. *(To Jenine.)* You want something from room service? Let me get you something from room service. *(To phone.)* Hello. Yeah. It's me. Right—Penthouse. Give me a coupla lobsters—caviar—yeah beluga—what do you think. And champagne— yeah. *(To Jenine.)* It's on its way. The best. I took care of it. *(To phone.)* Hello—Get me Letterman. Yeah. Letterman its me. Kiss my butt. What? *(Snorts and stamps.)* Fuck you, fuck you, fuck you. *(To Jenine.)* The food's on its way up. *(Beat.)* You asked me what's it like. It's thrilling. It's fantastic. I love it. This is it. This is it. Me. *(Beat.)* I see you looking at me. And I know what you're thinking. You want me to lay you. Hell. Get in line sweetie. Everybody wants me to lay them. Get in line sweetheart. Better yet, they want to screw me royally. Cause I'm on top. Hell. I can have anybody I want. Watch this. *(To phone.)* Hello— get me, uh—Hell. I've had them all…screw it. Call all of them. Tell them all to come up here and kiss my butt. *(Snorts and stamps.)* This is it. Hell. This is it. Hell. Hell. *(Snorts.)*

JENINE: Hell. This is it…

(Ext. Field.)

(Img. Road. City to country.)

(We hear wind.)

JENINE: When I was a little girl, Paradise was visiting my grandpa out in the country. And in the clearing of a grassy field, we'd catch falling stars— that turned into fireflies—caught them in preserve jars and carried them to our beds…

(Img. city scape.)

(We hear office sounds.)

JENINE: And I worked my way up at this woman's magazine. Finally got the promotion I've been working for. With a corner office with a view...

VOICE: But one day she got a postcard from Barbara.

(Img. Eiffel Tower with Bab's smile.)

JENINE: It could have been the postcard I got from Barbara.

BARBARA: They call me Babs. But my parents named me Babar. But I prefer Barbara. It makes it seem as if my parents were sane. If they were my parents. I met Jenine in college. Northwestern. I ran there—running away from home. College was a safe haven. We were liberal arts majors taking no brainer classes. All we had to do was repeat whatever the teachers said—like trained barking dogs.—Is the surface of the moon rough?— Ruff! Liberal arts majors. Honor roll students. We skipped most classes and went bowling or to the movies. If we could just step into that screen.

(Int. movie house.)

(We see flickering light and hear projector sound.)

BARBARA: I was in love with Spencer Tracey. During Christmas break I hitched all the way to California searching for him. He was already dead. I guess I should have known—But up there on the screen—you—know—he's so alive. That's what's so great about movies—movie stars—they just keep flickering up there they never die. If I could step inside the frame and it would be like— *(Katherine Hepburn imitation.)* "Hello Spencer—I'm your Katherine Hepburn now." Step in and out of different places—Africa...Japan...Step into a Bruce Lee flick. Bruce Lee's cute. He's dead too.

(We hear La Dolce Vita *music.)*

BARBARA: Or Fellinni. Jenine loved Fellinni—me too. I'd love to be like up there on the screen in La Dolce Vita and...I'd be Anita Eckberg doing a pagan dance at the ruins of the Baths of Carracalla. I love that dress she's wearing. So, I'd be dancing wildly in that dress at the ruins of the Baths of Carracalla and then—cut to—Marcello wading after me into the Trevi fountain—and then the camera would find me down some dark mysterious street and I'd have a kitten playing in my hair—We saw that movie at least twenty-two times.

JENINE: Twenty-five times. All through college, Barbara and I were joined at the—

BARBARA: ...hip. I visited her at her parent's house. That was wild.

(We hear Rufus' horn.)

BARBARA: Your father was playing Gabriels horn—I mean really loud. Can't hear a thing anybody says. And everything is covered in plastic.

Everything. Her mother wears a plastic apron and slippers. I was thinking, man, is she going to like serve fruit that looks real until you bite into it...I should be so lucky to have a family like Jenine. I was organically grown. At the commune, I had twelve fathers, thirty-four mothers and one hundred seventy-two siblings. When I was seven, Nirvana and Moonbeam—their real names are Bob and Hildy. I call them Bob and Hildy. It just kills them—took me with them out of the commune. Something about Utopia feeling cramped. They claimed to be my biological parents. But I've never been sure. I asked for blood tests. Hildy, she says she remembers labor pains. She can't swear that Bob is my father—but he was her favorite lay. But she definitely remembers labor pains. And she had taken some mushrooms right before her water broke. So things got a little distorted. She remembers pushing and pushing maybe hours—maybe days trying to give birth to something the size of, oh, a baby elephant—it felt like—and finally as she pushed it out. She looked down and sure enough an elephant's head was coming out between her legs—she says—that's why she named me Babar. She called me Babs. People, like, thought it was short for Barbara—and I didn't mind. After the commune, Bob and Hildy got rich doing EST seminars. They were always trying to get me to "open up," "free myself," "let it all hang out." But I refused. Even when Jenine came to visit me.

JENINE: All I remember is two buck-naked white people greeting me at the door.

BARBARA: Bob and Hildy served us raw organic carrots for thanksgiving dinner. I didn't say a word. I think this college thing is my way of rebelling. I think I'll become a housewife. I'll marry a doctor and vacuum and watch soaps all day and my husband will look like Spencer Tracey.—It would just kill them.

JENINE: Barbara met a doctor while in college and they got married and lived happily ever after until Spencer Tracey MD was killed in a drug deal gone bad. I don't think she ever recovered. She called me once saying...

BARBARA: I can't take it anymore. My parents are trying to get me to join some pilgrimage to become the bride of some Swami—so I'm going to run to France.

JENINE: I hadn't heard from her since then. Until I got this postcard. *(Jenine draws Barbara's postcard.)*

(Img. Eiffel Tower with Bab's smile.)

JENINE: She was sitting barefoot on an avenue—the Eiffel Tower behind her and something growing from her thigh. Exposed as casually as a garter—

what looked like a man growing from her thigh. It reads "Greetings from Paris."

(We hear Nina Rotta music.)

JENINE: And she's smiling.

(Int. office.)

(We hear typing, office sounds.)

JENINE: I went into the office the next day. My secretary—She's been spacing out a lot lately—and I don't know—maybe it was the postcard...

SECRETARY: She yelled at me—"Where do you go!" and I never knew I went anywhere—though she's not the first to call it to my attention. I'll be in the middle of a conversation—and I'm right there—I'm listening. I'm nodding my head—uh hm—uh hm...and I'm right there—folding clothes and my husband will say—"What did I just say Suzanne?" And I'll repeat the last thing I heard. And he'll say—"Where were you?" And I guess I'm doing this more frequently because more and more people ask me. And I don't know—I mean—I don't remember going anywhere. Its not like...There was this girl in high school—She'd come to class stoned. She'd say "present" at roll call and then the rest of the day she'd nod and smile and tap her foot. No one bothered her—not even the teachers and she didn't bother anyone...and she'd nod and smile and tap her foot. Well, her parents had been killed in a terrible accident. Me? I can't think of any tragedy in my life. And its not like I want to take any drugs—or have a desire to—But what if one day I just keep going—um hm—uh hm—and never come back...

JENINE: I meant to say Suzanne would you just snap out of it...It came out "WHERE DO YOU GO! TELL ME!" So, I took the rest of the day off and I went to the movies.

(Int. movie house.)

(We hear Nina Rotta music.)

JENINE: They were having a Fellinni festival—La Dolce Vita

(Projected video clip from the Fellinni film "La Dolce Vita" into close up of Marcello.)

JENINE: Marcello, who has my father's eyes, is searching for a more meaning-ful way of life. He most admires an intellectual writer named Steiner. Steiner seems to have a perfect life, a promising career, sterling wife and two children that he dotes on. Stimulating friends. Steiner seems too happy. Too fulfilled. One day he comes home—kills his two charming children and shoots himself in the head.

(We hear a clock strike three o'clock.)

JENINE: After the movie I went home. I packed one bag. By three a.m.—I was flying off to Italy and I said: I am leaving everything behind.

(Int. taxi.)

(We hear honking.)

TAXI DRIVER: FRICKING BASTARDS! Excuse my French. You OK? You didn't lose nothing did you? Fine. Good. Just hold on next time. That's what you gotta do.

(Maze—running in slow motion.)

(We hear wind.)

VOICE: How I Escaped Paradise. TAKE II.

(We hear a door slam.)

(We hear I'll Never Hear Bells music.)

VOICE: While flying over the Atlantic she dreams of the Wonderellas. And they said.

(Terrinikka, Karen, Ronnie and Terrinikka overlapping.)

TERRINIKKA: Why do you want to break up the group?

KAREN: Don't you know this is family.

RONNIE: And what's thicker than blood?

TERRINIKKA: Our harmonies are thick like blood.

VOICE: And she said.

JENINE: I could no longer tell whose voice was whose and whose was my own.

(I'll Never Hear Bells *music.)*

(Terrinikka, Karen, Ronnie overlapping.)

TERRINIKKA: Want to separate blood from the body.

KAREN: Running off.

RONNIE: Flying solo.

TERRINIKKA: She'll come crawling back.

KAREN: She'll come crawling back.

RONNIE: She'll come crawling back.

(Overlap sound of train and whistle.)

JENINE: Taking the train—There was nothing planned about this trip, take a train from the tip of Italy and work my way up the boot. I don't know what I was looking for except to experience the place, the food, the folk, the art, the architecture and the wines of Tuscany.

(We hear Nina Rotta music.)

(Img. map with red lines, overlap furry dice hanging from rearview mirror.)

(We hear car horn honking.)

TOUR GUIDE: Honk, Honk, Honk...Calabria is the boot toe and some people consider it to be the end of the earth...Basilecata stretches across Italy's instep...It is a mountainous region with large tracts of barren and eroded wasteland...Goethe said a man who has seen Naples can never be sad.

(Img. Rome postcard.)

TOUR GUIDE: The mind of the traveler is like a sleepwalker—you are in different places and times all at once. Walking around the ruins of Rome—I am also zig zagging around Manhattan. Honk, Honk, Honk—passing the ruins of the Bronx—I can hear Nero fiddling somewhere in the square.

JENINE: I walk down the Via Veneto searching for Fellinni. I want to ask him about La Dolce Vita, Steiner, the dead fish—Marcello's eyes—These mysteries...I guess what I really want to ask him is why my father never returned. *(Breathing.)*

(We hear wind.)

JENINE: My great great grandma was a slave—she had twenty-four children. Two sets of twins. My great grandma who was one of the first set of those twins. She and her twin had each twenty-two children. My grandma had only fourteen children. She wanted to keep the family small and refused to sleep with grandpa during the harvesting season, but couldn't deny to keep him warm in the winter. One day when she was pregnant with her fourteenth child grandma ran away from grandpa—out from the country and she never returned. "That was back when he had teeth." Was all grandma would say. My mother had three children.

(Img. parts of Jenine, Karen and Ronnie.)

(We hear Rufus' travel Music. Img. eyes.)

JENINE: My daddy Rufus endearingly called us each a waste of a good fuck. He was a musician.

RUFUS: My horn was my heaven. *(Plays horn.)* That there was called—three naked black men scrunched down—three naked niggers scrunched down underneath...three scared mother hubbards scrunched down underneath the backseat of a fire red Plymouth screeching out of the Mississippi Delta. You hear me—you know what I'm talking about—damn, you're a waste of a good fuck. You hear me—you got to be fast—hold onto your horn and blow. Got to be doubly fast—know what I'm

saying—In this world—Ain't talking about two four time. There's a space in between time. *(He plays.)* See. And in between is the air. You catch that air cause it will take you out. You flying once you grab hold to that air. The air in between. Hear me—They say sambo—and you— *(He blows.)* They say—boy, hoe that row— *(He blows.)* —And you out of there—you fast, you catch that freight train into oblivion—and you don't turn around—just keep on going. Nothing can touch you when you inside the music. Hear me Jenine? Hear me Jenine? Felt that way with your moms. Closest thing in this world was when I touched your moms—Insides her—and— *(He plays.)* —You hear me—ha—ha. *(We hear Rufus travel music.)*
(Img. clouds.)

JENINE: My Daddy's heaven was his horn. He traveled with Shades and Herman. They played bass and piano. The Three Gents. *(She draws.)* Daddy had just come back from a roadtrip to Nebraska, Missouri and Kansas. That summer he loaded us into the back of a pickup truck and we visited grandpa out in the country.
(We hear honking.)

JENINE: We took the Highway—honking all the way. Just outside the town that always smelled of—He'd lived alone those years since grandma took the children and ran. And he did have big white teeth—smiling and waving at us as we piled out of the back—me, my sister Karen, my brother Ronnie and my cousin Terrinikka. Us children feasted by the lake on stolen apples, a can of mackerel in oil and a can of peaches in heavy syrup brother Ronnie opened with a Swiss Army Knife—Daddy had brought him from Missouri. Then we laid down in the long sweet grass, our belly's to the sun watching dragons glide by puffing trails of smoke. Ran home through a cockle burr patch—Picked the burrs from each others feet. Nightfall—we laughed at the planets. And in the clearing of a grassy field, we caught falling stars that turned into fireflies—caught them in preserve jars and carried them to our beds.
(We hear Rufus travel music.)

JENINE: This was before my father took that road trip to Mississippi. He didn't come back the same. His face was a dark hard mask. He never said what happened on that road trip and he never went back on the road. But, went deeper and deeper inside his music. Days would pass before he came back.

RUFUS: *(Plays.)* Hear me Jenine—you hear me. Taking the air.

JENINE: I think I felt what he meant when we sang.

(Song—I'll Never Hear The Bells.)

JENINE: Me, my cousin Terrinikka, my brother Ronnie, and my sister Karen formed a singing group called the Wonderellas and we dressed up like the Shirelles and the Supremes. And we were so jealous of Ronnie.

RONNIE: That was before my voice changed—because I had the prettiest legs. They were all knees. And our harmonies were thick like blood. Nothing could come between us. Even when mamma...

MADEAR: ...Discovered my only son dressed in my shoes and wig and looking pretty enough to slap. *(She slaps Ronnie. Ronnie holds face.)*

JENINE: We stopped dressing up.

(Song—I'll Never Hear The Bells.)

JENINE: But you could still hear our voices 'til three A.M. on a Friday night.

(We hear Rufus' horn screech...clock ticking.)

JENINE: And mama started closing windows—drawing the shades in the dead of summer. And putting plastic over everything. The couch, chairs, the T.V....dining tables...

MADEAR: ...waiting for the man I married to come back.

(Rufus' horn turns into Nina Rotta music.)

(Ext. Rome.)

(We hear car honking.)

TOUR GUIDE: Honk, Honk, Honk...The Via Veneto is filled with ghosts. Passing the church of Santa Maria della Concezione...

JENINE: We come to the ruins of the Baths of Carracalla—and see my barefoot girlfriend Barbara.

(Img. Barbara's smile.)

(La Dolce Vita music.)

BARBARA: I love it when you call me Barbara. It sounds so normal. I know my head is shaved and my dead lover is attached to my thigh. My Spencer Tracey M.D. It didn't turn out as I imagined. When he was gunned down by the feds—or the pigs as Bob and Hildy say—there went my paradise. They impounded everything. Everything. I wandered a bit. Went back home—which had moved to Florida. Hildy and Bob were running a sun-worshipping retreat there. I thought I was getting skin cancer. It started out as a small growth on my thigh. Hildy and Bob think all illness is psychosomatic. We make our own joy, sadness— heaven, hell. So we chanted over my leg. O.K., I was desperate, Jenine. But the damn thing kept growing like some displaced penis. It was growing out of my thigh. Well, I began to think—of the possibilities...It kept growing...then I could see it was taking the shape of my dead husband.

My Spencer Tracey M.D. At this point we had tried faith healers...a woman—Sister Sinclair suggested I pluck out my eyes—like out of sight out of mind...Bob and Hildy were pushing me to join some pilgrimage. That's when I ran to Europe—and became a UBIST at the University of UBU. I am now an avowed UBU CULTIST. They taught me to accept myself as I am. Accept what life has given me—accept the baggage of my life. So at first I thought. O.K.—if I accept Bob and Hildy screwing me up so bad that I have something growing out of me, letting it all hang out—if I accept my prince charming was really a drug dealing toad—if I just accept then it will all go away—my parents, this growth—everything will disappear—and I'll be free and happy—and live ecstatically for the rest of my life. But you know—accepting is accepting. So, here I am. Did you get my postcard?

JENINE: She then swings the appendage growing from her thigh over her shoulder and takes my hand leading me down back to the Via Veneto. *(Img. red lines of map over Barbara's smile.)*

BARBARA: Some people—you can read their life on their face—like a map—me *(Indicates appendage.)*...and I get paid for it. People take snapshots—me and the Eiffel Tower. So one day this guy, I guess a talent scout, takes my picture and gives it to Fellinni—and he casts me in "The Ship Sails On"—It wasn't a featured part—I was one of the extras. But I was in for a moment. A flickering moment.

(We hear clock ticking.)

JENINE: And she's smiling.

(We hear clock strike three o'clock.)

VOICE: Her last evening in Rome...Jenine writes—in a small room with a naked lightbulb—postcards to loved ones she left behind.

JENINE: *(Writing.)* Here I am taking metropolitan vigil
#365. Torn postcards of the mecca/wasteland.
Sifting through the piled on debris to uncover
women making love with breastplates on and men
in helmets. Loose cabbages singing
hymns on street corners, saluting
a poor child who passes in pee-stained
pajamas, sleepwalking, barefootedly
maneuvering down cobblestone avenues
and narrow cracked-out playgrounds.
Some day I will write a book entitled
how I escaped paradise

and dedicate it to my barefoot
girlfriend, Barbara, who ran
to a city in Europe, whose legends
include that of Antoinette, the holy
Antoinette, who took a razor to her head
and cut off her long tresses in penance
only to have them grow back overnight
and so it went until she scraped and
scraped—till slicing crosses
in her head—she sat in the middle
of the townsquare weeping
like the confused, bald,
bleeding babe that she was.
When her skull lay bare
the cry of anarchist arose
and she was burned.
They keep her ashes and her hair
in a glass encasement in the center
of the town to attract flashbulb-tourists
with thick-clumsy tongues.
They smile lizard-like when passing.

Here, Barbara ran, to escape the dead lover attached to her thigh. And here she remains to this day, studying with a noted Ubist at the University of Ubu. She herself an avowed Ubucultist. She chants in fluent Ubu now. Oh, holy Barbara.

How did I get in here. I said I was leaving everything behind. But I find myself here in this room revisiting ghosts...Dead memories—forgotten loved ones...

(Img. legs.)

JENINE: He made me laugh—my brother Ronnie—we laughed and laughed and laughed—I hadn't laughed like that in a long time. Since...I can't remember when...He visited me in California—He'd left home shortly after I did. He said...

RONNIE: I was tired of hiding. You know I'm still pretty enough to slap. I want to know, Jenine, why you hadn't come home for daddy's funeral. *(Pause.)* I went home last year for cousin Ester's wedding. I love cousin Ester 'cause she could work miracles with some hair. And I went home for her wedding dressed as Natalie Cole, don't you know sistergirl, I had the nerve to get up and sing—

(Song—Natalie Cole's Inseparable.*)*

RONNIE: And nobody recognized me—not even Mama. "My voice may have dropped but." *(Snap.)*

JENINE: And he laughed and laughed telling me about cousin Ester's wedding…I loved laughing with Ronnie…*(Pause.)* How did I get here? I had packed one bag leaving everything behind. Get the next plane ticket. Land in Italy. Take a train from the tip of Italy and work my way up the boot. I don't know what I was looking for…except to experience the place, the food, the folk, the art, the architecture…The wines of Tuscany.

(O Patria Mia music.)

JENINE: Walking around Florence reminded me of an opera set and I knew any minute people would step out on the balconies and start singing arias…

(We hear wind.)

JENINE: *(Breathing.)* …my grandma had only fourteen. She refused to sleep with my grandpa during the harvesting seasons…but couldn't deny to keep him warm in the winter…and my mother had three children. Me, my brother—Ronnie, and my twin sister Karen.

(Img. Karen's arms.)

KAREN: Steven and I are going to Martha's Vineyard to vacation this summer. We always take five weeks each year to vacation. Last year we went to Switzerland. And, oh, the skiing there was just fabulous. Though I almost froze my black butt off. *(She laughs.)* "My black butt off"—That sounds like something cousin Ester would say.

COUSIN ESTER: Girl, git yo' black butt on over here.

KAREN: Remind me to tell you a story about my cousin Ester—

JENINE: When we were girls before we had known the full weight of a man—that inevitably divides sisters one from another with—"You think you pretty or something—you bow-legged—

KAREN: Baboon breathed—

JENINE: Elephant-footed, nappy headed, rotten-toothed—still wetting the bed and blaming it on me, with your pee-stained, yellow holey drawers wearing—

KAREN: I'll snatch you bald—looking at my man when you know he saw me first."

JENINE: —accusations. But when we were white-shirted—Plaid skirted—girls, my sister and I were inseparable and knew nothing could come between us. Such was the nature of our love.

KAREN: My cousin Ester's wedding. I swear, my relatives. I don't speak to half of them anymore. At least half. My Aunt Rose comes up to me...

AUNT ROSE: Girl, you act like you don't want to talk to nobody. What's wrong with you?

KAREN: Aunt Rose, please, I barely speak to my own mother twice a year, why would I want to speak with you more frequently? She never called. She never wrote. Not even a card for my wedding. And I did send her an invitation. So you know how us Negroes are—C.P. time. The Reverend was late to the church. My cousin Ester is panicking. Everyone is outside the church waiting. The bridesmaids—everybody is there. The wedding party's colors are purple and lime. So, anyway, Stanley, that's Ester's betrothed, picks the lock of the church. How he knows how to pick that lock, don't ask me. Everybody's in the church. The Reverend finally arrives. He was stuck in traffic on the bus. The bus.

(Song—Inseparable.)

KAREN: Ester had some woman, some relation to her lock-picking husband to be's family, singing Natalie Cole's

(Ronnie: singing Inseparable.)

KAREN: Who ever told that woman she could sing...She's just wailing as loud as can be. And my cousin Terrinikka who is somewhere in the back— the one with the gold across her front teeth inscribed with her initials, is going—

TERRINIKKA: Goddamn, sang it girl! Sang it!

KAREN: This is in church in the middle of a wedding service. Steven, my husband, and I are losing it. He's having a great time. He had never seen anything like this before in his life. Steven is a buppie from birth. I had to work for it.

TERRINIKKA: Gaddamn, sang it girl!

KAREN: With her initials—T.I.T.—Terrinikka Imogene Thompson— inscribed in gold across her front teeth. My husband looks around at my relatives and says, "Doggone sweetheart, I guess I got the pick of the litter with you, huh?" (We hear song "Stop in the name of love.")

(Img. Magritte-like fragmented body parts.)

JENINE: It was in my family that I felt whole. More whole even though I was always the child with my father's eyes, my mother's mouth, someone else's disposition and attitude and soon. No part of me was mine but with my family the puzzle fit.

(Img. slides of body parts of family.)

JENINE: This was before my sister got lost in the looking glass and she never returned. My brother found himself inside the body of a pretty black woman—and he never returned. My mother—plastic.

(We hear a screeching sound.)

JENINE: Before my father took that trip to Mississippi...

(Img. shadows.)

JENINE: And that ones called three scared mother fuckers scrunched down in the back seat of a fine red Plymouth screeching out of the goddamn mother fucking Mississippi delta.

(Img. Florence.)

(O Patria Mia music.)

JENINE: Walking around Florence reminded me of an opera set and I knew any minute people would step out on the balconies and start singing arias. I felt like I was in a Fellinni movie. And the huge, bigger than life statues—Dante...surrounded...Everywhere you go are people who look like those statues. Italians are beautiful. Earthy friendly people. And the men—You walk into la Trattoria—I bought an English/Italian dictionary. Che cose la specialita della casa pre favor? "Oh, no problemo." Everyone, no matter what...Could you direct me to the Boboli Gardens?—"Oh, no problemo." To anything—"No problemo." Can you tell me, per favore, la direzione...This guy with coal black curly hair in a business suit on a moped—at a stop light—"I'm looking for the Uffezzi—"Oh, no problemo." He takes me there. I'm riding on the back of his moped—holding on for dear life hoping I don't lose my legs on the side of a car. These narrow streets and back alleys...takes me to the front door. "Il Uffezzi—no problemo,—Ciao Bella." Everywhere you go—"Ciao Bella." That's all. And he rides away. I'm in love with Italy. I'm in love.

(We hear three knocks.)

(Int. the house that Jack built.)

(We see a shadow. Caption—Jack's house)

JENINE: I knew it the moment I saw him. I knew he was the one.

(We hear a bell ring.)

JENINE: My husband Jack sold real estate.

(We hear a second ring.)

VOICE: Paradise is a walled in garden.

JENINE: I worked at an elementary.

(Jenine stands at drawing easel.)

(We hear a third ring.)

(Int. school.)

JENINE: Rebecca, that was perfect, you get a gold star. Billy, you get a silver star. You'll do better next time.

(Int. house.)

JENINE: We lived in a nice middle class neighborhood.

(We hear clock ticking.)

JENINE: Jack was a good man. A hard worker. He had our existence mapped out according to the ten year plan. A thirty year mortgage—we would sell in two and a half years—and he had already drafted out our dream house—we would build it on the white mountains of Utah. In three years we would start a family. A boy and then a girl. He was constantly closing the deal. "Honey, We're closing the deal" "Closing the deal."

VOICE: Paradise is a walled garden.

JENINE: He calculated strategies for job promotions. Measured the distance between arm chair to kitchen. He timed orgasms. He weighed his emotions. He plotted the course of our lives with an even and fair hand.

(Ticking stops.)

JENINE: He was a good man. I got pregnant in three years into our ten year plan. I ate and ate and rolled around like a fat happy Buddha—my husband worshiping my belly—where our son grew inside me. I was fat and full of life and happy. We lived in the fortress that Jack built—There I would have my perfect son...my perfect husband...me.

(We hear wind.)

JENINE: Taking the air. *(She breathes.)* My grandma had only fourteen...she refused...

(We hear thunderous rain.)

JENINE: THE NIGHT MAMA CALLED TO SAY DADDY HAD STOPPED TAKING THE AIR—I LOST THE CHILD.

(Img. mother's open mouth.)

(Rufus' travel music.)

VOICE: Remembering the room with the coffin—Madear, in plastic flowered bathrobe and slippers, sits in chair covered with plastic. On the lamp sits her wig. On top of the coffin is a glass of water with dentures. The wall of the room reads:

MADEAR: *(Reading wall:)*

Rufus swung
his face at last to the wind
and then his neck snapped.

Your father, Rufus—was the seventh son of a seventh son. His horn was his heaven. But he called me his light. His pillar. But he had some jealous eyes he never wanted me going nowhere by myself and spent most of his offtime fighting some man that looked like he was looking in my direction. But he would never raise a finger to harm a hair on my head. Though sometimes it felt like he was strangling the life out of me. So deep was his love. "And such is the nature of love," he said. So I stayed with him and never veered my eyes right or left or any other direction that wasn't his way. So deep was my love for him and such is the nature of love. Rufus. Hmm. Rufus…Didn't want to buy you that horn. Your mama, she knew. Could feel it in you. Had always known even before she pushed you out and licked you clean, she knew. Hmm. Like I knew with each of mine. Could see through to their bones' marrow before I even smelled or tasted them. Now they all gone. All of them. What's known is known and still you can't do nothing about it. All you can do is what you can and then sit back and watch as they run their own course. Nothing to be done. No, didn't want to buy you that horn. On account of musicians way leads you the long and side way. His daddy said and his daddy knew the way of needles that musicians is prone to. But Rufus was gonna play—horn or no—it was in his blood…And he was fast—mercurial—could play in between the music. Took me my first time when I was fifteen and had my first child that same year. We—Yes! He could play. Could play me. Yes! When he touched me—well…Did I say…Always was moody. That was given even before the smack oozed through his pores.

(We hear lip-splitting jazz riff.)

MADEAR: 1964. He came back from that road trip. His face—he turned his face from me—He came back and his face was this hard wooden mask—with slits for eyes. He was never the same. Never told me what happened on that road trip…three black men traveling through Mississippi… 1964.

(Img. Feet in chains.)

(We hear O Patria Mia.)

MADEAR: After that the sounds from his horn was…something fearful. He never told me what happened on that road trip. Then on when he touched me—hmm. My throat aches for the old times.

(We hear clock strike three o'clock.)

JENINE: *(Writing.)* Three am. I could hear the rhododendrons swaying in the forest and the three black men scrunched in the backseat of the fire-red Plymouth screeching out of the Mississippi delta. He used to be mercurial as he traveled from armchair to kitchen to my mother's bedroom where I could hear them shouting in the middle of the night—equations more frightening than the dead angel I had stuffed between my mattresses. Tonight rounding the city corner I fell into a hole of mating locusts. They deposited their larva in my ears. Within the cocoon they sang—Wala—eeee—Rushing up the highway—the ambulance stopped a moment to pick up the blood-splattered feathers.

Years after the long hot summer.

I never return

for the winters

nor listen

to the mosquitoes

gnawing on the pavement.

(We hear a school bell.)

JENINE: Class repeat after me...She never returns...Billy—that wasn't perfect but I'm going to give you three gold stars—for effort...

(Int. house.)

JENINE: This is the maiden of the farm that milked the cow with the crooked horn that tossed the dog over the barn that chased the cat that killed the rat that ate the malt that lay in the house that Jack built...This is the man all tattered and torn that kissed the maiden of the farm...This is the priest all shaved and shorn that married the man all tattered and torn. *(Jenine slices her wrists.)*

SECRETARY: Umm hmm...umm hmm...

TAXI DRIVER: You O.K.? You didn't lose nothing did you? You just gotta hold on next time—That's what you gotta do.

BABS: Some people you can read their life on their face like a map...me...

SUPERSTAR: Hell...this is it...Hell—

(Rufus blows his horn that stop on an intake.)

JENINE: Where do you go?...

GROUP: Want to separate blood from the body—Running off—Flying solo...She'll come crawling back.

(Jenine falls to floor lifeless.)

VOICE: How I Escaped Paradise—TAKE III.

(We hear a door slam.)

(Song—Rolling On The River.)

TERRINIKKA: I always wanted to be the second Ikette on the left. Even before I wanted to be a mortician. Way back in high schools at LG Pinkston in Dallas, Texas—in the West Dallas Projects where I grew up. My cousin Jenine would take me downtown to Hall Street to the joints and listen to Bobby McKeeler and his band play. And me and my cousin we would dance like we was boyfriend and girlfriend. And then afterwards we would go out with Bobby McKeeler and his band and 'nem—cause my cousin went to elementary with Bobby at George Washington Carver—and we'd get some of that mesquite Bar-B-Q and go over the bridge to pick up some beers and hang out over at the lake with Bobby 'nem. And Bobby would tell us about his cousin. Well they weren't first cousins like me and Jenine—more like his aunt's second cousin was how Bobby became blood to Ike of Ike and Tina Turner. And Bobby always said, when Ike and Tina Turner came through town he was going to introduce us to them. And we always said when they did and he introduced us, we was going to pack our bags and run off, you know—hit the road with Ike and Tina Turner and become the second and third Ikette on the left. I felt, even then—that that was my calling. Well, I graduated from high school and worked at the Bar-B-Q shack—Jenine...I haven't heard from her in ages. She's over in...Germany...Sent me a postcard once. And I studied for my mortician's license. Fixing up dead folk is something I truly enjoy. I wouldn't say it was my calling—My friends didn't understand at all.

FRIEND: Terrinikka, you must be crazy. You're so full of life—how can you stand to be touching up on them dead people?

TERRINIKKA: And I tell them it's something I'm good at. I got a feel for what I'm doing. I love making dead folk look like they're alive again.

(Song—Rolling On A River.)

TERRINIKKA: But I know my real calling is the second Ikette on the left. 'Cause when Ike starts up to playing and Tina and us start doing the do—We got the power to raise the dead. Folks walking around in life like they dead already—come alive again. That's my calling.

(As Terrinikka—dances high heels stomping in syncopation-faster-and faster doing a whirligig. We hear a clock strike three o'clock. Jenine runs in slow motion.)

VOICE: Three A.M. and she was still running...

JENINE: After I bled all over the white walls and carpet in the house that Jack built—I ran to California—searching for signs...The thread...

(We hear a horn honking.)

ALTHEA: (Taxi driver.) ...clickin my fricken heels...

JENINE: ...Honking all the way to grandpa's house...

(Nina Rotta music.)

TOUR GUIDE: Ah Venezia. It is truly a city of romance. You are surrounded by water. Il Canales Grandes Gondolas—sleek black hearses draped in oriental rugs—canopies—old cantores serenading enchanted lovers as beautiful gondoliers steer upon mirrors of water as if doing a tango. Two steps and they dip their oars as if lowering a shy virgin into the sea.

JENINE: By the time I reached Venice…the trek up the boot had been like a dream. By now, I couldn't tell the difference. Venice is such a fantastical city. Walking down a narrow alley that opens into the vastness of San Marcos Plaza—three o'clock on a Sunday morning—pigeons fluttering in the square. I look up at the bell tower as two naked Moors beat out the hours. Naked deities look down from the buildings, palace and church. The church hallway is inlaid with mosaics and murals—an intricate layering of Roman, African and Oriental influences. A congregation prays to deities crafted centuries ago by the finest artists of the day. Art is life and life is art and I am walking in a waking dream of smells, sounds, colors, textures—among the dark eyed, raven haired…A Tunisian student stranded here after a civil war shadows me through the plaza. Inside the palace his face is mirrored in the carved mahogany doors……Crossing over the Bridge of Sighs…I find myself on Lido Island. A long tongue of an island. The beach was immortalized in Thomas Mann's—Death in Venice. On this beach is a rocky lower lip thrust out into the ocean. I walk out onto the lip and the ocean licks at my legs on either side. Night falls—

(Img. Venice.)

JENINE: —and I take the ferry back to Venice. I hear a gravely voice behind me as I touch land. "Ciao Bella." And a massive rough hand lightly touches my back. I turn and a granite-like satyr of a man stands before me. His skin is alabaster—broad shoulders and tall. He's speaking to me. I'm speechless because I think I'm dreaming and he must know I'm saying "yes" by reading my eyes. We walk back into the heart of Venice. Venice is a maze. A labyrinth of intricate passages. I've constantly lost my way. He leads with a sureness. He walks like a bull. I don't know where he came from. Had he been watching me since Lido? He appeared from nowhere…

(Img. eye of a horse.)

(Light up on Madear.)

MADEAR: Now, see, I know I come from another generation all together but some things I just don't understand. You bear a child—raise them up good. That's all you can do, really. And then one day they come to you and they don't recognize their own. Like they don't remember where they come from. Well, excuse my headrag but you come from this here black woman's womb. All of ya'll trying to deny it now and seeking comfort in the arms of strangers.

(Light change.)

(Img. shadows become reflections.)

JENINE: ...We drank cappucinos and then wine. Drawing on a note pad to fill in where our words break off. He draws a kitchen and a man—himself. He's a cook he says. Somehow I don't believe him. Late into the night we walk around a square listening to tapes. I put in Aida—but he prefers to listen to Ike and Tina Turner. We are in a plaza dancing to Ike and Tina Turner. He stamps and snorts like a minotaur.

(Img. muscles of a horse become water.)

JENINE: In the room. He lifts me up—undressing me Am I awake. Awake enough to look for my dictionary.—Rubbers...Rubbers...Rubbers...Prophylactics...There are no words for sex or sex paraphernalia in my dictionary—Damn. I draw a rubber. He snorts with laughter. "Si, Si. No problemo." And lifts me up again. He does not give—not one inch of him gives. He is made of stone. I climb on top. We move like water.

(Img. light/shadow shifting.)

JENINE: My mind is a maze—I've turned this corner before. Something familiar about this passageway. The pigeon screams—impaled upon the monument. My tongue is unrecognizable. Whose teeth are these. What hand is touching my navel. I search for the key and find it in the door. I turn to say goodnight. He's gone.

(We see a shaft of light/ door slam.)

VOICE: Paradise is a one night stand.

(We hear a clock strike three o'clock.)

JENINE: Three A.M. in the morning...The moon is a blood red knife. The stars braille. Alone in this room rocking back and forth on stained sheets—listening to the drunken accusations of ghosts—of forgotten loved ones who hang by their feet from the bedposts and swing the canopy in the morning breeze.

For my father—his horn was his heaven.

My mother tried to preserve hers in plastic.

My sister lost her self in the looking glass.

My brother found himself inside the body of a pretty black woman.

Sister Sinclair took out her eyes so that she could see paradise without any distractions.

and Barbara took another way

and Terrinikka...and...and...umm hmm...umm hmm...umm hmm.

some people stay fixed in one moment replaying the same old record.
Some people give up on the idea—
But I keep going out on the road.
(Img. water.)

JENINE: Here I am taking metropolitan #365—and it always seems to be back when and over there: I keep running—looking for that elusive mercurial...something. Like trying to catch the minotaur by the tail. It keeps changing locations—changing forms. Holding onto a piece of thread— I go forward and back—and sideways and back again—The path to that job and the family a safe place—and money and power and sex...a flickering moment. And even if I do get there and capture it—by morning all I have are dead fireflies rolling around in the bottom of a jar. I long to shed everything. Memories, expectations and becoming nothing but air—taking flight I take flight and begin again—collecting those voices— and people—places, smells, sounds, colors, textures—In between—back when and over there. It seems that its not in the arrival—and holding onto; it's in the journey.
(Img. reflection of water.)

JENINE: Where to—where to—which way do you want me to go?
I have come to this land—and no air
Where crouching humans breathe
in dust filled corners and close their eyes
Shutter-like against mirror and wind.
Where, below, landscapes and horizons stretch out
like a lazy dog soaking up the sun.
Lunatics line the highway like signposts.
Honking all the way to grandpa's house.
Just outside the town that always smelled
of...He's lived alone
these years since grandma took the children
and ran, (back when he had teeth.)
and she never returned.
He waves and smiles a pink-gum smile
inviting me into the tin-topped cave.
Chickens peck on the roof like rain.
(Img. Grandpa's dentures in glass of water.)

JENINE: Grandpa,
do you remember summers
when we'd drive down

and eat from your garden
and the well water was so bitter
and you'd let us shoot the gun?
(We hear cicadas.)
(Img. open sky and stars.)
JENINE: I pull over to the side of the road.
Grandpa asleep
his head on the dashboard
drunken spittle sliding down
his chin. Too many tamales
and tequilas. Cicadas
droning all around. I squat
in the clearing
of a grassy field. Open
my eyes as scorching
fireflies
dash blindly
against my face.
(Door opens. Jenine exits. Black out)

END OF PLAY